LEARN FRENCH WITH ROMANTIC STORIES

isbn: 978-1-987949-75-9

Dear Reader and Language Learner!

You're reading the Kindle learner edition of our Bermuda Word pop-up e-books which we sell at learn-to-read-foreign-languages.com. Before you start reading French, please read this explanation of our method.

Since we want you to read French and to learn French, our method consists primarily of word-for-word literal translations, but we add idiomatic English if this helps understanding the sentence. For example for French:

Il y avait du vin
It there had of the wine
[There was wine]

This method works best if you re-read the text until you know the high frequency words just by reading, and then mark and learn the low frequency words in your reader or practice them with our brilliant App.

Don't forget to take a look at the e-book App with integrated learning software that we offer at learn-to-read-foreign-languages.com! For more info check the last two pages of this e-book!

Thanks for your patience and enjoy the story and learning French!

Kees van den End

TABLE   DES   MATIÈRES
TABLE   OF THE   CONTENTS

Guy   de   Maupassant   (1850-1893)
Guy   de   Maupassant

Émile   Zola   (1840-1902)
Émile   Zola

Maupassant   -   LE   BONHEUR   -   Première   Partie   -   4
Maupassant   THE   HAPPINESS   First   Part

Maupassant   -   LE   BONHEUR   -   Deuxième   Partie   -   20
Maupassant   THE   HAPPINESS   Second   Part

Maupassant   -   LA   CONFESSION   -   47
Maupassant   THE   CONFESSION

Zola   -   LE   CARNET   DE   DANSE   -   71
Zola   THE   NOTEBOOK   OF   DANCE
              [THE   BALLROOM   DIARY   ]

Maupassant   -   SOUVENIR   -   98
Maupassant   MEMORY

Zola   -   UN   BAIN   - 130
Zola   A   BATH

Guy   de   Maupassant   -   LE   BONHEUR
Guy   de   Maupassant   THE   HAPPINESS

Première   partie
First   part

C'était   l'heure   du   thé,   avant   l'entrée   des   lampes.
It was   the hour   of the   tea   before   the entrance   of the   lamps
          (the time)   (for)   (the bringing in)

La   villa   dominait   la   mer;   le   soleil   disparu   avait   laissé
The   villa   dominated   the   sea   the   sun   disappeared   had   left
              (had an overview of)   (which had disappeared)

le   ciel   tout   rose   de   son   passage,   frotté   de   poudre
the   sky   all   pink   of   her   passage   rubbed   in   powder

d'or;   et   la   Méditerranée,   sans   une   ride,   sans   un   frisson,
of gold   and   the   Mediterranean   without   a   wrinkle   without   a   shiver
                                                    (ripple)

lisse,   luisante   encore   sous   le   jour   mourant,   semblait   une
smooth   shiny   still   under   the   day   dying   seemed   a

plaque   de   métal   polie   et   démesurée.
plate   of   metal   polished   and   disproportionate
                                    (huge)

Au (In the) **loin,** (distance) **sur** (on) **la** (the) **droite,** (right) **les** (the) **montagnes** (mountains) **dentelées** (with teeth (serrated))

dessinaient (drew) **leur** (their) **profil** (profile) **noir** (black) **sur** (on) **la** (the) **pourpre** (purple) **pâlie** (paled (pale)) **du** (of the)

couchant. (laying down (sunset))

On (One (They)) **parlait** (spoke) **de** (of) **l'amour,** (the love) **on** (one (they)) **discutait** (discussed) **ce** (this) **vieux** (old) **sujet,** (topic) **on** (one (they))

redisait (said again) **des** (of the (the)) **choses** (things) **qu'on** (that they) **avait** (had) **dites,** (said) **déjà,** (already) **bien** (good (quite)) **souvent.** (often)

La (The) **mélancolie** (melancholy) **douce** (sweet) **du** (of the) **crépuscule** (dusk) **ralentissait** (slowed) **les** (the) **paroles,** (words)

faisait (made) **flotter** (float) **un** (a) **attendrissement** (softening) **dans** (in) **les** (the) **âmes.** (souls)

7 Le Bonheur I

Et ce mot: "amour" , qui revenait sans cesse, tantôt
And this word love that returned without stop sometimes

prononcé par une forte voix d'homme, tantôt dit par une
pronounced by a strong voice of man sometimes spoken by a
(of a man)

voix de femme au timbre léger, paraissait emplir le petit
voice of (a) woman in the tone light appeared to fill the small

salon, y voltiger comme un oiseau, y planer comme un
salon and to flutter as a bird and hover as a

esprit.
ghost

Peut-on aimer plusieurs années de suite?
Can one love several years of following
(in) (a row)

"Oui," prétendaient les uns.
Yes claimed the ones
[some]

"Non," affirmaient les autres.
No affirmed the others
[others]

On distinguait les cas, on établissait des démarcations,
They distinguished the cases, they established of the demarcations
()

on citait des exemples.
they quoted of the examples
(the)

Et tous, hommes et femmes, pleins de souvenirs
and all men and women full of memories

surgissants et troublants, qu'ils ne pouvaient citer et qui
popping up and troubling that they not could call out and that

leur montaient aux lèvres, semblaient émus, parlaient de
them rose to the lips appeared moved spoke of

cette chose banale et souveraine, l'accord tendre et
this thing banal and sovereign the agreement tender and

mystérieux de deux êtres, avec une émotion profonde et
mysterious of two beings with an emotion deep and

un intérêt ardent.
an interest ardent

9 Le Bonheur I

Mais tout à coup quelqu'un, ayant les yeux fixés au
But all at strike someone having the eyes fixed in the
(of a) (sudden)

loin, s'écria:
distance exclaimed

"Oh! voyez, là-bas, qu'est-ce que c'est?"
Oh see there down what is it that it is

Sur la mer, au fond de l'horizon, surgissait une masse
On the sea in the background of the horizon arose a mass

grise, énorme et confuse.
gray huge and confused

Les femmes s'étaient levées et regardaient sans
The women themselves were lifted and watched without
(had) (stood up)

comprendre cette chose surprenante qu'elles n'avaient
understanding this thing surprising that they not had

jamais vue.
never seen
(ever)

10 Le Bonheur I

Quelqu'un dit:
Someone *said*

"C'est la Corse! On l'aperçoit ainsi deux ou trois fois
It is *the* *Corsica* *One* *it discerned* *like this* *two* *or* *three* *times*
()

par an dans certaines conditions d'atmosphère
by *year* *in* *certain* *conditions* *of atmosphere*
(in a)

exceptionnelles, quand l'air d'une limpidité parfaite ne la
exceptional *when* *the air* *of a* *clarity* *perfect* *not* *it*

cache plus par ces brumes de vapeur d'eau qui voilent
hides *more* *with* *these* *mists* *of* *vapor* *of water* *that* *veil*

toujours les lointains."
always *the* *distances*
(distant places)

On distinguait vaguement les crêtes, on crut reconnaître
One *distinguished* *vaguely* *the* *ridges* *one* *thought* *to recognize*
(mountain ridges)

la neige des sommets.
the *snow* *of the* *peaks*

11   Le Bonheur I

Et — And
tout — all [everyone]
le — the]
monde — world
restait — remained
surpris, — surprised
troublé, — troubled
presque — almost
effrayé — frightened

par — by
cette — this
brusque — abrupt
apparition — apparition
d'un — of a
monde, — world
par — by
ce — this
fantôme — phantom

sorti — come out
de — of
la — the
mer. — sea

Peut-être — Maybe
eurent-ils — had they
de — of ()
ces — these
visions — visions
étranges, — strange
ceux — those
qui — that

partirent, — left
comme — just like
Colomb, — Columbus
à travers — through
les — the ()
océans — oceans
inexplorés. — unexplored

Alors — Then
un — an
vieux — old
monsieur, — gentleman
qui — who
n'avait — not had (had)
pas — not
encore — yet
parlé, — spoken

prononça: — said

"Tenez,   j'ai   connu   dans   cette   île,   qui   se   dresse   devant
Hold   I have known   in   this   island that itself raises   in front of
(Wait)   (on)

nous,   comme   pour   répondre   elle-même   à   ce   que   nous
us   as if   for   to reply   her self   to this that we

disions   et   me   rappeler   un   singulier   souvenir,   j'ai   connu
were saying and me   to remind of a   singular   memory   I have   known

un   exemple   admirable   d'un   amour   constant,   d'un   amour
an   example   admirable   of a   love   constant   of a   love

invraisemblablement   heureux.   Le   voici."
improbably   happy   It   see-here
                                 [Here it   is]

"Je   fis,   voilà   cinq   ans,   un   voyage   en   Corse."
I   made   see-there   five   years   a   trip   in   Corsica
              (you know)   (years ago)   (on)

13   Le Bonheur I

"Cette île sauvage est plus inconnue et plus loin de
This island wild is more unknown and more far from

nous que l'Amérique, bien qu'on la voie quelquefois des
us than the America well that one it sees sometimes from the
         (America) (even though)

côtes de France, comme aujourd'hui."
coasts from France as today

"Figurez-vous un monde encore en chaos, une tempête
Imagine yourself a world still in chaos a storm

de montagnes que séparent des ravins étroits où roulent
of mountains that separate of the ravines narrow where roll
                         () (run)

des torrents; pas une plaine, mais d'immenses vagues de
of the torrents not a plain but of immense waves of
()   (immense)

granit et de géantes ondulations de terre couvertes de
granite and of giant ripples of earth covered of
       ()   (with)

maquis ou de hautes forêts de châtaigniers et de pins."
dense shrubs or of high forests of chestnut trees and of pines
         (with)   ()

"C'est un sol vierge, inculte, désert, bien que parfois on
It is an earth virgin uncultivated deserted well that sometimes one
(even though)

aperçoive un village, pareil à un tas de rochers au
notices a village similar to a heap of rocks at the

sommet d'un mont."
top of a mountain

"Point de culture, aucune industrie, aucun art."
Nothing of culture no industry no art

"On ne rencontre jamais un morceau de bois travaillé,
One not encounters never a piece of wood worked
(ever) (carved)

un bout de pierre sculptée, jamais le souvenir du goût
an end of stone sculpted never the memory of the taste

enfantin ou raffiné des ancêtres pour les choses
childish or refined of the ancestors for the things
( )

gracieuses et belles."
graceful and beautiful

15 Le Bonheur I

"C'est là même ce qui frappe le plus en ce superbe
It is there even that which strikes the most in this superb
(precisely) (one)

et dur pays:"
and hard country

"l'indifférence héréditaire pour cette recherche des formes
the indifference hereditary for this search of the forms

séduisantes qu'on appelle l'art."
attractive that one calls the art

"L'Italie, où chaque palais, plein de chefs-d'œuvre, est un
The Italy where each palace full of masterpieces is a
(Italy)

chef-d'œuvre lui-même, où le marbre, le bois, le bronze,
masterpiece itself where the marble the wood the bronze

le fer, les métaux et les pierres attestent le génie de
the iron the metals and the stones attest the genius of

l'homme."
the man
(man)

"Où   les   plus   petits   objets   anciens   qui   traînent   dans   les
Where   the   most   small   objects   old   that hang around   in   the

vieilles   maisons   révèlent   ce   divin   souci   de   la   grâce,   est
old   homes   reveal   this   divine   care   of   the   gracefulness is

pour   nous   tous   la   patrie   sacrée   que   l'on   aime   parce
for   us   all   the   homeland   sacred   that   it one   loves   because

qu'elle   nous   montre   et   nous   prouve   l'effort,   la   grandeur,
that she   us   shows   and   us   proves   the effort   the   greatness

la   puissance   et   le   triomphe   de   l'intelligence   créatrice."
the   power   and   the   triumph   of   the intelligence   creative

"Et,   en   face   d'elle,   la   Corse   sauvage   est   restée   telle
And   in   face   of her   the   Corsica   wild   is   remained   such
                             ()

qu'en   ses   premiers   jours.   L'être   y   vit   dans   sa   maison
that in   her   first   days.   The being   there   lives   in   its   house

grossière,   indifférent   à   tout   ce   qui   ne   touche   point   son
coarse   indifferent   to   everything   this   which   not   touches   not at all   its

existence   même   ou   ses   querelles   de   famille."
existence   itself   or   its   quarrels   of   family
                                   [family quarrels   ]

17 Le Bonheur I

"Et il est resté avec les défauts et les qualités des
And he is remained with the defects and the qualities of the
(has)

races incultes, violent, haineux, sanguinaire avec
races uncultivated violent hateful bloodthirsty with

inconscience, mais aussi hospitalier, généreux, dévoué, naïf,
unawareness but also hospitable generous devoted naive

ouvrant sa porte aux passants et donnant son amitié
opening his door to the passersby and giving his friendship

fidèle pour la moindre marque de sympathie."
faithful for the littlest sign of sympathy

"Donc depuis un mois j'errais à travers cette île
So since a month I wandered across this island

magnifique, avec la sensation que j'étais au bout du
magnificent with the feeling that I was at the end of the
(beautiful)

monde."
world

"Point d'auberges, point de cabarets, point de routes."
Nothing / of inns / nothing / of / cabarets / nothing / of / roads

"On gagne, par des sentiers à mulets, ces hameaux
One / gains (reaches) / by / of the () / trails / for / mules / these / hamlets

accrochés au flanc des montagnes, qui dominent des
clung (clinging) / to the / flank / of / mountains / that / dominate / of the

abîmes tortueux d'où l'on entend monter, le soir, le bruit
abysses / tortuous / from where it one (one) / hears / rising up / the / evening / the / noise

continu, la voix sourde et profonde du torrent."
continuous / the / voice / muffled / and / deep / of the / torrent

"On frappe aux portes des maisons."
One / knocks / at the / doors / of the / homes

19 Le Bonheur I

"On demande un abri pour la nuit et de quoi vivre
One requests a shelter for the night and of [some what food to live]

jusqu'au lendemain."
until (the) next day

"Et on s'asseoit à l'humble table, et on dort sous
And one sits down at the humble table and one sleeps under

l'humble toit; et on serre, au matin, la main tendue de
the humble roof and one presses (shakes) at the (in the) morning the hand reached out of

l'hôte qui vous a conduit jusqu'aux limites du village."
the host who you has led up to the edge of the village

Guy   de   Maupassant   -   LE   BONHEUR

Guy   de   Maupassant   THE   HAPPINESS

Deuxième   partie

Second   part

Or,	un	soir,	après	dix	heures	de	marche,	j'atteignis	une
Now	one	evening	after	ten	hours	of	travel	I attained (I reached)	a

petite	demeure	toute	seule	au	fond	d'un	étroit	vallon	qui
small	abode	all	alone	at the	background	of a	narrow	vale	that

allait	se	jeter	à	la	mer	une	lieue	plus	loin.	Les	deux
was going	itself	to throw (to finish)	at	the	sea	one	league	more [farther	further away]	The	two

pentes	rapides	de	la	montagne,	couvertes	de	maquis,	de
slopes	fast (steep)	of	the	mountain	covered	of (with)	dense shrubs	of (with)

rocs	éboulés	et	de	grands	arbres,	enfermaient	comme
rocks	tumbled down	and	of (with)	great	trees	closed in	like

deux	sombres	murailles	ce	ravin	lamentablement	triste.
two	dark	walls	this	ravine	miserably	sad

Autour   de   la   chaumière,   quelques   vignes,   un   petit   jardin,
Around   of   the   cottage   some   grapevines   a   small   garden

et   plus   loin,   quelques   grands   châtaigniers,   de   quoi   vivre
and   more   further   some   great   chestnut trees   of   what   to live
[farther   away]   [as   livelyhood   ]

enfin,   une   fortune   pour   ce   pays   pauvre.
finally   a   fortune   for   this   country   poor
(all in all)

La   femme   qui   me   reçut   était   vieille,   sévère   et   propre,
The   woman   that   me   received   was   old   severe   and   clean

par   exception.
by   exception

L'homme,   assis   sur   une   chaise   de   paille,   se   leva   pour
The man   sat   on   a   chair   of   straw   himself rose   for
(rose)

me   saluer,   puis   se   rassit   sans   dire   un   mot.   Sa
me   to welcome   then   himself   sat down again   without   to say   a   word   His

compagne   me   dit:
companion   (to) me   said

"Excusez-le; il est sourd maintenant. Il a quatre-vingt-deux
Excuse   him he is (deaf)mute now   He has four-twenty-two
                                              (is) (eighty)

ans."
years
(years old)

Elle parlait le français de France. Je fus surpris.
She   spoke   the French   of France   I   was surprised

Je lui demandai:
I   her asked

"Vous n'êtes pas de Corse?"
You   not are not of Corsica

Elle répondit:
She   replied

"Non; nous sommes des continentaux. Mais voilà
No we are of the continentals But see there
(continent) (that is)

cinquante ans que nous habitons ici."
fifty years that we live here

Une sensation d'angoisse et de peur me saisit à la
A feeling of anguish and of fear me seized at the

pensée de ces cinquante années écoulées dans ce trou
thought of these fifty years passed in this hole

sombre, si loin des villes où vivent les hommes.
dark, so far of the cities where live the men

Un vieux berger rentra, et l'on se mit à manger le
An old shepherd returned, and it one oneself put to eat the
() (started)

seul plat du dîner, une soupe épaisse où avaient cuit
only dish of the dinner, a soup thick where had cooked

ensemble des pommes de terre, du lard et des choux.
together of the potatoes the bacon and of the sprouts
(pommes de terre; apples of earth) () ()

25 Le Bonheur II

Lorsque le court repas fut fini, j'allai m'asseoir devant la
When the short meal was over I went to seat myself in front of the
(to sit down)

porte, le cœur serré par la mélancolie du morne
door the heart tight by the melancholy the dreary

paysage, étreint par cette détresse qui prend parfois les
landscape embraced by this plight that takes sometimes the
()

voyageurs en certains soirs tristes, en certains lieux
travelers in certain nights sad in some locations

désolés.
desolate

Il semble que tout soit près de finir, l'existence et
It appears that everything would be close of to end the existence and

l'univers.
the universe

On perçoit brusquement l'affreuse misère de la vie,
One perceives abruptly the terrible misery of the life

l'isolement de tous, le néant de tout, et la noire
the isolation of all the nothingness of everything and the black

solitude du cœur qui se berce et se trompe lui-même
solitude of the heart that cradles and deceives itself

par des rêves jusqu'à la mort.
by of the dreams up until the death
()   ()

La vieille femme me rejoignit et, torturée par cette
The old woman me joined and tortured by this

curiosité qui vit toujours au fond des âmes les plus
curiosity that lives always at the background of the souls the most

résignées:
resigned

"Alors vous venez de France?" dit-elle.
Then you come from France said she

"Oui, je voyage pour mon plaisir."
Yes I travel for my fun

"Vous êtes de Paris, peut-être?"
You are from Paris maybe

"Non, je suis de Nancy."
No I am from Nancy

Il me sembla qu'une émotion extraordinaire l'agitait.
It me seemed that an emotion extraordinary her agitated

Comment ai-je vu ou plutôt senti cela, je n'en sais rien.
How | have I | seen | or | rather | felt | that | I | not of it | know | nothing

Elle répéta d'une voix lente:
She | repeated | of a (with a) | voice | slow

"Vous êtes de Nancy?"
You | are | from | Nancy

L'homme parut dans la porte, impassible comme sont les
The man | appeared | in | the | door | impassive | as | are | the

sourds.
deafmute

29   Le Bonheur II

Elle **reprit:**
She   continued

"Ça **ne** **fait** **rien.**
That   not   does   nothing

Il **n'entend** **pas."**
He   not hears   not

Puis, **au** **bout** **de** **quelques** **secondes:**
Then   at the   end   of   some   seconds

"Alors **vous** **connaissez** **du** **monde** **à** **Nancy?"**
Then   you   know   of the   world   in   Nancy

"Mais   oui,   presque   tout   le   monde."
But   yes   almost   all   the   world
                             [everybody   ]

"La   famille   de   Sainte-Allaize?"
The   family   of   Saint   Allaize

"Oui,   très   bien;   c'étaient   des   amis   de   mon   père."
Yes   very   good   they were   of the friends of   my   father
                                      ()

"Comment   vous   appelez-vous?"
How   you   call   yourself

Je   dis   mon   nom.
I   told   my   name

Elle me regarda fixement, puis prononça, de cette voix
She me looked at fixedly then uttered in this voice

basse qu'éveillant les souvenirs:
low that wakes up the memories

"Oui, oui, je me rappelle bien. Et les Brisemare,
Yes yes I me recall well And the Brisemare

qu'est-ce qu'ils sont devenus?"
what is this that they are become

"Tous sont morts."
All are dead

"Ah! Et les Sirmont, vous les connaissiez?"
Ah And the Sirmont you them would know

"Oui,   le   dernier   est   général."
Yes   the   last   is   general

Alors   elle   dit,   frémissante   d'émotion,   d'angoisse,   de   je   ne
Then   she   said   shaking   of emotion   of anguish   of   I   not

sais   quel   sentiment   confus,   puissant   et   sacré,   de   je   ne
know   what   feeling   confused   powerful   and   sacred   of   I   not

sais   quel   besoin   d'avouer,   de   dire   tout,   de   parler   de
know   what   need   to confess   of   to say   everything   of   to speak   of

ces   choses   qu'elle   avait   tenues   jusque-là   enfermées   au
these   things   that she   had   kept   until there locked   in the

fond   de   son   cœur,   et   de   ces   gens   dont   le   nom
background   of   her   heart   and   of   these   people   which   the   name
(depth)

bouleversait   son   âme:
upset   her   soul

"Oui, Henri de Sirmont. Je le sais bien."
Yes   Henri   of   Sirmont   I   him   know   well

"C'est mon frère."
It is   my   brother

Et je levai les yeux vers elle, effaré de surprise.
And   I   raised   the   eyes   to   her   aghast   of   surprise

Et tout d'un coup le souvenir me revint.
And   all   of a   strike   the   memory   me   returned
                    (sudden)

Cela avait fait, jadis, un gros scandale dans la noble
That   had   made   back then   a   big   scandal   in   the   noble

Lorraine.
Lorraine

Une jeune fille, belle et riche, Suzanne de Sirmont,
A young girl beautiful and wealthy Suzanne of Sirmont,

avait été enlevée par un sous-officier de hussards du
had been taken by an under officer of Hussars of the

régiment que commandait son père.
regiment that commanded her father.

C'était un beau garçon, fils de paysans, mais portant
It was a beautiful boy son of peasants but wearing

bien le dolman bleu, ce soldat qui avait séduit la fille
good the dolman blue this soldier who had seduced the girl

de son colonel.
of his colonel.

Elle l'avait vu, remarqué, aimé en regardant défiler les
She him had seen noticed loved in watched parade the

escadrons, sans doute.
squadrons no doubt.

35   Le Bonheur II

Mais comment lui avait-elle parlé, comment avaient-ils pu
But how him had she spoken how had they been able

se voir, s'entendre? comment avait-elle osé lui faire
eachother to see to get together how had she dared him make
[to see eachother]

comprendre qu'elle l'aimait? Cela, on ne le sut jamais.
understand that she loved him That one not it knew never
() (would know)

On n'avait rien deviné, rien pressenti. Un soir, comme
One not had nothing guessed nothing sensed in advance One evening as
(People) (had)

le soldat venait de finir son temps, il disparut avec
the soldier came of to finish his time he disappeared with

elle. On les chercha, on ne les retrouva pas. On n'en
her They them sought they not them found not They not of it
() ()

eut jamais des nouvelles et on la considérait comme
had never of the news and they her considered as
(ever)

morte.
dead

Et   je   la   retrouvais   ainsi   dans   ce   sinistre   vallon.
And   I   her   rediscovered   thus   in   this   sinister   vale

Alors   je   repris   à   mon   tour:
Then   I   resumed   in   my   turn

"Oui,   je   me   rappelle   bien.   Vous   êtes   mademoiselle
Yes   I   me   recall   well   You   are   miss

Suzanne."
Suzanne

Elle   fit   "oui" ,   de   la   tête.   Des   larmes   tombaient   de   ses
She   did   yes   of   the   head   Of the   tears   fell   from   her
(made a sign of)   (with)   ()

yeux.   Alors,   me   montrant   d'un   regard   le   vieillard   immobile
eyes   Then   me   showing   of a   look   the   old man   immobile
(with a)

sur   le   seuil   de   sa   masure,   elle   me   dit:
on   the   threshold   of   his   hovel   she   me   said

"C'est   lui."
That is   him

Et   je   compris   qu'elle   l'aimait   toujours,   qu'elle   le   voyait
And   I   understood   that she   loved him   always   that she   him   saw

encore   avec   ses   yeux   séduits.
still   with   his   eyes   seducing

Je   demandai:
I   asked

"Avez-vous   été   heureuse   au   moins?"
Have   you   been   happy   at the   least
                                          (at)

Elle   répondit,   avec   une   voix   qui   venait   du   cœur:
She   replied   with   a   voice   that   came   from the heart

"Oh! oui, très heureuse. Il m'a rendue très heureuse. Je
Oh　yes　very　happy　　He　me has　rendered　very　happy　　I
　　　　　　　　　　　　　　　　　(made)

n'ai jamais rien regretté."
not have　never　nothing　regretted

Je la contemplais, triste, surpris, émerveillé par la
I　her　contemplated　sad　surprised　marveled　by　the
　　　　　　　　　　　　　　　　　(marveling)

puissance de l'amour!
power　of　the love

Cette fille riche avait suivi cet homme, ce paysan.
This　girl　wealthy　had　followed　this　man　this　peasant

Elle était devenue elle-même une paysanne.
She　was　become　her self　a　peasant
　　(had)

Elle   s'était   faite   à   sa   vie   sans   charmes,   sans   luxe,
She   herself was   made   to   his   life   without   charms   without   luxury
      (had)   (adapted)

sans   délicatesse   d'aucune   sorte,   elle   s'était   pliée   à   ses
without   delicacy   of none at all   kind   she   herself was   bent   to   his
                        (had)

habitudes   simples.
habits   simple

Et   elle   l'aimait   encore.
And   she   loved him   still

Elle   était   devenue   une   femme   de   rustre,   en   bonnet,   en
She   was   become   a   woman   of   rusticness   in   cap   in
      (had)

jupe   de   toile.
skirt   of   linen

Elle mangeait dans un plat de terre sur une table de
She ate in a dish of earth on a table of
(from)

bois, assise sur une chaise de paille, une bouillie de
wood sat on a chair of straw a porridge of

choux et de pommes de terre au lard.
sprouts and of apples of earth at the bacon
(in)

Elle couchait sur une paillasse à son côté.
She slept on a bench at his side

Elle n'avait jamais pensé à rien, qu'à lui!
She not had never thought to nothing than to him

Elle n'avait regretté ni les parures, ni les étoffes, ni
She not had regretted nor the adornments nor the fabrics nor

les élégances, ni la mollesse des sièges, ni la tiédeur
the elegances nor the softness of the seats nor the warmness

parfumée des chambres enveloppées de tentures, ni la
fragrant of the rooms wrapped of drapes nor the
(in)

douceur des duvets où plongent les corps pour le repos.
softness of the duvets where plunge the bodies for the rest

Elle n'avait eu jamais besoin que de lui; pourvu qu'il
She not had had never need than of him; provided that he
provided
(as long as)

fût là, elle ne désirait rien.
was there she not wanted nothing

Elle   avait   abandonné   la   vie,   toute   jeune,   et   le   monde,
She   had   abandoned   the life   all   young   and the world

et   ceux   qui   l'avaient   élevée,   aimée.
and those that her had   esteemed loved

Elle   était   venue,   seule   avec   lui,   en   ce   sauvage   ravin.
She   was   come   alone   with   him   in   this wild   ravine
       (had)

Et   il   avait   été   tout   pour   elle,   tout   ce   qu'on   désire,
And he   had   been everything for her   everything this that one desires

tout   ce   qu'on   rêve,   tout   ce   qu'on   attend   sans   cesse,
everything this that one dreams everything this that one awaits without cease

tout   ce   qu'on   espère   sans   fin.
everything this that one hopes without end

43   Le Bonheur II

Il	avait	empli	de	bonheur	son	existence,	d'un	bout	à
He	had	filled	of (with)	happiness	her	existence	from one	end	to

l'autre.
the other

Elle	n'aurait	pas	pu	être	plus	heureuse.
She	not would	not	been able	to be	more	happy

Et	toute	la	nuit,	en	écoutant	le	souffle	rauque	du
And	all	the	night	in	listening	the	breath	hoarse	of the

vieux	soldat	étendu	sur	son	grabat,	à	côté	de	celle
old	soldier	stretched out	on	his	pallet	to the	side	of	that one (her)

qui	l'avait	suivi	si	loin,	je	pensais	à	cette	étrange	et
who	him had	followed	so	far	I	thought	to (of)	this	strange	and

simple	aventure,	à	ce	bonheur	si	complet,	fait	de	si
simple	adventure	to (of)	this	happiness	so	complete	made	of	so

peu.
little

44 Le Bonheur II

Et je partis au soleil levant, après avoir serré la main
And I left at the sun rising after to have closed the hand
(shaken)

des deux vieux époux.
of the two old spouses

II
II

Le   conteur   se tut.   Une   femme   dit:
The   storyteller   fell silent   A   woman   said

"C'est   égal,   elle   avait   un   idéal   trop   facile,   des   besoins
It is   equal   she   had   an   ideal   too   easy   of the   needs
(It doesn't)   (matter)

trop   primitifs   et   des   exigences   trop   simples.   Ce   ne
too   primitive   and   of the   requirements   too   simple   This   not
                           ()

pouvait   être   qu'une   sotte."
could   be   than a   fool

Une   autre   prononça   d'une   voix   lente:
An   other   uttered   of a   voice   slow
                            (with a)

"Qu'importe!   elle   fut   heureuse."
Whatever   it   was   happy

Et   là-bas,   au   fond   de   l'horizon,   la   Corse   s'enfonçait
And   there down   at the   back   of   the horizon   the   Corsica   sank
                                 (in the)   ()

dans   la   nuit,   rentrait   lentement   dans   la   mer,   effaçait   sa
in   the   night   returned   slowly   in   the   sea   erased   its
                                                          (to)

grande   ombre   apparue   comme   pour   raconter   elle-même
big   shadow   appeared   as   for   to tell   her   self

l'histoire   des   deux   humbles   amants   qu'abritait   son   rivage.
the history   of   two   humble   lovers   that housed   its   shore

47   Le Bonheur II

Guy de Maupassant - LA CONFESSION
Guy   de   Maupassant   THE   CONFESSION

Marguerite de Thérelles allait mourir. Bien qu'elle n'eût
Marguerite   de   Thérelles   went   to die   Good   that she   not had
(was going)   (Although)

que cinquante et six ans, elle en paraissait au moins
(more) than   fifty   and   six   years   she   of it   appeared   at the   least
()

soixante et quinze. Elle haletait, plus pâle que ses
sixty   and   fifteen   She   panted   more   pale   than   her
[seventyfive   ]

draps, secouée de frissons épouvantables, la figure
sheets   shaken   of   chills   frightening   the   figure

convulsée, l'œil hagard, comme si une chose horrible lui
convulsed   the eye   haggard   as   though a   thing   horrible   her
()

eût apparu.
had   appeared
(appeared before her)

Sa sœur aînée, Suzanne, plus âgée de six ans, à
Her   sister   elder   Suzanne   more   old   of   six   years   at

genoux près du lit, sanglotait.
(the) knees   close   of the   bed   sobbed

Une petite table approchée de la couche de l'agonisante
A small table put close to the bed of the dying

portait, sur une serviette, deux bougies allumées, car on
carried on a napkin two candles alight because they

attendait le prêtre qui devait donner l'extrême-onction et
awaited the priest who had to give the extreme unction and
(the sacrament)

la communion dernière.
the communion last

L'appartement avait cet aspect sinistre qu'ont les chambres
The apartment had this appearance sinister that have the rooms

des mourants, cet air d'adieu désespéré. Des fioles
of the dying this ambiance of farewell desperate Of the vials
() ()

traînaient sur les meubles, des linges traînaient dans les
were left on the furniture of the cloths were left in the
() ()

coins, repoussés d'un coup de pied ou de balai. Les
corners moved away of a kick of (the) foot or of broom The
(with a)

sièges en désordre semblaient eux-mêmes effarés, comme
seats in disorder appeared themselves frightened as

s'ils avaient couru dans tous les sens.
if they had ran in all the directions
()

51 La Confession

La redoutable mort était là, cachée, attendant.
The fearsome death was there hidden waiting

L'histoire des deux sœurs était attendrissante. On la citait
The history of the two sisters was touching On it quoted

au loin; elle avait fait pleurer bien des yeux.
from the afar she had made cry good of the eyes
(from) (many)

Suzanne, l'aînée, avait été aimée follement, jadis, d'un
Suzanne the eldest had been loved madly back then by a

jeune homme qu'elle aimait aussi. Ils furent fiancés, et
young man that she loved too They were engaged and

on n'attendait plus que le jour fixé pour le contrat,
one not awaited more than the day set for the contract
(wedding)

quand Henry de Sampierre était mort brusquement.
when Henry of Sampierre was dead abruptly
(had) (died)

Le désespoir de la jeune fille fut affreux, et elle jura
The despair of the young girl was awful and she swore

de ne se jamais marier.
of not herself never to marry
() (ever)

Elle tint parole. Elle prit des habits de veuve qu'elle
She held word She took of the clothes of widow that she
()

ne quitta plus.
not took off anymore

Alors sa sœur, sa petite sœur Marguerite, qui n'avait
Then her sister her small sister Marguerite who not had

encore que douze ans, vint, un matin, se jeter dans
yet (more) than twelve years came one morning herself threw in

les bras de l'aînée, et lui dit: "Grande sœur, je ne
the arms of the eldest and her said Big sister I not

veux pas que tu sois malheureuse. Je ne veux pas
want not that you are unhappy I not want not

que tu pleures toute ta vie. Je ne te quitterai jamais,
that you cry all your life I not you will leave never

jamais, jamais! Moi, non plus, je ne me marierai pas.
never never Me not anymore I not myself will marry not
(also) ()

Je resterai près de toi, toujours, toujours, toujours."
I will stay close of you always always always

Suzanne l'embrassa attendrie par ce dévouement d'enfant,
Suzanne her kissed touched by this dedication of child
(childish)

et n'y crut pas.
and not there believed not
(not it)

Mais la petite aussi tint parole et, malgré les prières
But the little one also kept word and, in spite of the prayers

des parents, malgré les supplications de l'aînée, elle ne
of the parents in spite of the supplications of the eldest she not

se maria jamais. Elle était jolie, fort jolie; elle refusa
herself married never She was pretty very pretty she refused

bien des jeunes gens qui semblaient l'aimer; elle ne
good of the young people that appeared to love her she not
(a good number)

quitta plus sa sœur.
left anymore her sister

Elles vécurent ensemble tous les jours de leur, existence,
They lived together all the days of their existence

sans se séparer une seule fois. Elles allèrent côte à
without themselves separate a single time They went side by

côte, inséparablement unies.
side inseparably united

Mais *But* **Marguerite** *Marguerite* **sembla** *seemed* **toujours** *always* **triste,** *sad* **accablée,** *overwhelmed* **plus** *more*

morne *depressed* **que** *than* **l'aînée** *the eldest* **comme** *as* **si** *though* **peut-être** *can-be (maybe)* **son** *her* **sublime** *sublime*

sacrifice *sacrifice* **l'eût** *her had* **brisée.** *broken* **Elle** *She* **vieillit** *aged* **plus** *more* **vite,** *fast* **prit** *took (got)* **des** *of the ()*

cheveux *hairs (hair)* **blancs** *whites (white)* **dès** *starting from* **l'âge** *the age* **de** *of* **trente** *thirty* **ans** *years* **et,** *and* **souvent** *often*

souffrante, *was unwell* **semblait** *seemed* **atteinte** *gripped* **d'un** *of a* **mal** *disease* **inconnu** *unknown* **qui** *that* **la** *her*

rongeait. *gnawed*

Maintenant *Now* **elle** *she* **allait** *went* **mourir** *to die* **la** *(as) the* **première.** *first*

Elle *She* **ne** *not* **parlait** *spoke* **plus** *anymore* **depuis** *since* **vingt-quatre** *twentyfour* **heures.** *hours* **Elle** *She* **avait** *had*

dit *said* **seulement,** *only* **aux** *at the* **premières** *first* **lueurs** *lights* **de** *of* **l'aurore:** *the daybreak*

"Allez chercher monsieur le curé, voici l'instant."
Come on look for mr the priest see here the instant
[right now]

Et elle était demeurée ensuite sur le dos, secouée de
And she was remained subsequently on the back shaken of

spasmes, les lèvres agitées comme si des paroles
spasms the lips agitated as if of the words
( )

terribles lui fussent montées du cœur, sans pouvoir sortir,
terrible her were mounted from the heart without power to come out

le regard affolé d'épouvanté, effroyable à voir.
the look panicked with fear appalling to see

Sa sœur, déchirée par la douleur, pleurait éperdument, le
Her sister torn by the pain cried madly the

front sur le bord du lit et répétait:
front on the board of the bed and repeated

"Margot, ma pauvre Margot, ma petite!"
Margot my poor Margot my little

Elle **l'avait** **toujours** **appelée:** **"ma** **petite"** **,** **de** **même** **que**
She   her had   always   called   my   little   of   same   that

la **cadette** **l'avait** **toujours** **appelée:** **"grande** **sœur."**
the   junior   her had   always   called   big   sister

On **entendit** **des** **pas** **dans** **l'escalier.** **La** **porte** **s'ouvrit.**
One   heard   of the   steps   in   the staircase   The   door   itself opened
()

Un **enfant** **de** **chœur** **parut,** **suivi** **du** **vieux** **prêtre** **en**
A   child   of   (the) choir   appeared   followed   by the   old   priest   in

surplis. **Dès** **qu'elle** **l'aperçut,** **la** **mourante** **s'assit** **d'une**
choir dress   From   that she   saw him   the   dying   sat upright   of a
(From the moment)   (with a)

secousse, **ouvrit** **les** **lèvres,** **balbutia** **deux** **ou** **trois**
jerk   opened   the   lips   stammered   two   or   three

paroles, **et** **se** **mit** **à** **gratter** **ses** **ongles** **comme** **si** **elle**
words   and   herself   put   to   scratch   (with) her   fingernails   as   if   she
[started]

eût **voulu** **y** **faire** **un** **trou.**
had   wanted   there   to make   a   hole

L'abbé **Simon** **s'approcha,** **lui** **prit** **la** **main,** **la** **baisa** **sur**
The father   Simon   approached   her   took   the   hand   her   kissed   on

le **front** **et,** **d'une** **voix** **douce:**
the   front   and   of a   voice   soft
(with a)

"Dieu vous pardonne, mon enfant; ayez du courage, voici
God you forgive my child have of the courage see here

le moment venu, parlez."
the moment (has) come talk

Alors, Marguerite, grelottant de la tête aux pieds,
Then Marguerite shivering from the head to the feet

secouant toute sa couche de ses mouvements nerveux,
shaking all her bed of her movements nervous

balbutia:
stammered

"Assieds-toi, grande sœur, écoute."
Seat yourself big sister listen

Le prêtre se baissa vers Suzanne, toujours abattue au
The priest himself lowered to Suzanne always downcast at the
(still)

pied du lit.
foot of the bed

La   releva,   la   mit   dans   un   fauteuil   et,   prenant   dans
Her   raised   her   put   in   a   chair   and   taking   in

chaque   main   la   main   d'une   des   deux   sœurs,   il
each   hand   the   hand   a one   of the   two   sisters   he

prononça:
spoke

"Seigneur,   mon   Dieu!   envoyez-leur   la   force,   jetez   sur
Lord   my   God   send   them   the   force   throw   on

elles   votre   miséricorde."
them   your   mercy

Et   Marguerite   se   mit   à   parler.   Les   mots   lui   sortaient
And   Marguerite   herself   put   to   speak   The   words   her   went out
                    [started]

de   la   gorge   un   à   un,   rauques,   scandés,   comme
from   the   throat   one   by   one   hoarse   chanted   as if
                                                    (measured spoken)

exténués.
exhausted

"Pardon,   pardon,   grande   sœur,   pardonne-moi!   Oh!   si   tu
Forgiveness   forgiveness   big   sister   forgive   me   Oh   if   you

savais   comme   j'ai   eu   peur   de   ce   moment-là,   toute   ma
knew   how   I have   had   fear   of   this   moment there all   my

vie! ..."
life

59   La Confession

Suzanne balbutia, dans ses larmes:
Suzanne stammered in her tears

"Quoi te pardonner, petite? Tu m'as tout donné, tout
What you forgive little (little one) You me have everything given all

sacrifié; tu es un ange..."
sacrificed you are an angel

Mais Marguerite l'interrompit:
But Marguerite her interrupted

"Tais-toi, tais-toi! Laisse-moi dire... ne m'arrête pas.... C'est
Silence yourself silence yourself Leave me to tell not stop me not It is
[Be quiet] [be quiet]

affreux... laisse-moi dire tout... jusqu'au bout, sans
awful leave me to say everything until the end not

bouger... Écoute.... Tu te rappelles... tu te rappelles...
move Listen You yourself remember you yourself remember

Henry..."
Henry

Suzanne tressaillit et regarda sa sœur. La cadette reprit:
Suzanne started and looked at her sister The junior continued

"Il faut que tu entendes tout pour comprendre. J'avais
It is necessary that you hear everything for to understand I had (was)

douze ans, seulement douze ans, tu te le rappelles
twelve years only twelve years you yourself it remember

bien, n'est-ce pas? Et j'étais gâtée, je faisais tout ce
well not is this not And I was spoiled I did everything this

que je voulais! ... Tu te rappelles bien comme on me
that I wanted You yourself remember well how they me

gâtait? ... Écoute.... La première fois qu'il est venu, il
spoiled Listen The first time that he is come he

avait des bottes vernies; il est descendu de cheval
had of the () boots varnished he is (has) descended from (his) horse

devant le perron, et il s'est excusé sur son costume,
in front of the steps and he himself is (himself has) excused on (for) his costume

mais il venait apporter une nouvelle à papa."
but he came bring a news to dad

"Tu te le rappelles, n'est-ce pas? ... Ne dis rien...
You yourself it remember not is this not Not say nothing
[You remember it, don't you]

écoute. Quand je l'ai vu, j'ai été toute saisie, tant je
listen When I him have seen I have been all gripped so much I

l'ai trouvé beau, et je suis demeurée debout dans un
him have found beautiful and I am remained upright in a

coin du salon tout le temps qu'il a parlé. Les enfants
corner of the salon all the time that he has spoken The children

sont singuliers... et terribles.... Oh! oui... j'en ai rêvé!"
are singular and terrible Oh yes I of it have dreamed

"Il est revenu... plusieurs fois... je le regardais de tous
He is come back several times I him watched of all
(with)

mes yeux, de toute mon âme... j'étais grande pour mon
my eyes from whole my soul I was big for my
(with)

âge... et bien plus rusée qu'on ne croyait. Il est
age and well more cunning that one not believed He is
(knew)

revenu souvent.... Je ne pensais qu'à lui."
come back often I not thought but to him
(but of)

"Je   prononçais   tout   bas:"
I   uttered   all   low
                        (very)   (soft)

" Henry...   Henry   de   Sampierre!   "
Henry   Henry   of   Sampierre

"Puis   on   a   dit   qu'il   allait   t'épouser.   Ce   fut   un   chagrin...
Then   one   has   said   that he   was going to marry you   This   was   a   grief
          (they) (have)

oh!   grande   sœur...   un   chagrin...   un   chagrin!   J'ai   pleuré
oh   big   sister   a   grief   a   grief   I have   cried

trois   nuits,   sans   dormir.   Il   revenait   tous   les   jours,
three   nights   without to sleep   He   returned   all   the   days

l'après-midi,   après   son   déjeuner...   tu   te   le   rappelles,
the afternoon   after   his   lunch   you   yourself it   remember

n'est-ce   pas!   Ne   dis   rien...   écoute.   Tu   lui   faisais   des
not is this this   not   Not   say nothing listen   You   him   made   of the

gâteaux   qu'il   aimait   beaucoup...   avec   de   la   farine,   du
cakes   that he   loved   a lot   with   of   the   flour   of the
                                                          ()   ()   ()

beurre   et   du   lait....   Oh!"
butter   and   of the milk   Oh
                  ()

"Je sais bien comment.... J'en ferais encore s'il le fallait.
I know well how I of it would make more if he it needed

Il les avalait d'une seule bouchée, et puis il buvait un
He them swallowed of a single bite and then he drank a
(with a)

verre de vin... et puis il disait: *C'est* *délicieux.* Tu
glass of wine and then he said *This is* *delicious* You

te rappelles comme il disait ça?"
yourself remember how he said that

"J'étais jalouse, jalouse! ... Le moment de ton mariage
I was jealous jealous The moment of your marriage

approchait. Il n'y avait plus que quinze jours. Je
approached It there not had more than fifteen days I
[It was not]

devenais folle. Je me disais: Il n'épousera pas Suzanne,
became crazy I myself said He not will marry not Suzanne
( )

non, je ne veux pas! ... C'est moi qu'il épousera, quand
no I not want not It is me that he will marry when

je serai grande. Jamais je n'en trouverai un que j'aime
I will be big Never I not of it shall find one that I love

autant..."
so much

"Mais un soir, dix jours avant ton contrat, tu
But one evening ten days before your marriage you

t'es promenée avec lui devant le château, au clair de
yourself are walked with him in front of the castle in the clear of
(have walked) (light)

lune... et là-bas... sous le sapin, sous le grand sapin...
(the) moon and there down under the fir under the big fir tree

il t'a embrassée... embrassée... dans ses deux bras... si
he you has embraced embraced in his two arms so

longtemps.... Tu te le rappelles, n'est-ce pas! C'était
long You yourself it remember not is this not This was

probablement la première fois... oui.... Tu étais si pâle
probably the first time yes You was so pale
(were)

en rentrant au salon!"
in returning to the salon

"Je vous ai vus; j'étais là, dans le massif. J'ai eu
I you have seen I was there in the bushes I have had

une rage! Si j'avais pu, je vous aurais tués! Je me
a rage If I had been able I you would have killed I myself

suis dit:"
am said
(have)

"'Il n'épousera pas Suzanne, jamais! Il n'épousera
He not will marry not () Suzanne never He not will marry

personne. Je serais trop malheureuse... ' . Et tout d'un
no-one I would be too unhappy And all of a [suddenly

coup je me suis mise à le haïr affreusement."
blow] I myself am put [started] to him hate horribly

"Alors, sais-tu ce que j'ai fait? ... écoute. J'avais vu le
Then know you this that I have done listen I had seen the

jardinier préparer des boulettes pour tuer des chiens
gardener prepare of the () little balls (pieces of meat) for to kill of the () dogs

errants. Il écrasait une bouteille avec une pierre et
stray He crushed a bottle with a stone and

mettait le verre pilé dans une boulette de viande."
put the glass pounded in a ball of meat

"J'ai pris chez maman une petite bouteille de
I have taken with (from) mom a small bottle of

pharmacien, je l'ai broyée avec un marteau, et j'ai
pharmacist I it have crushed with a hammer and I have

caché le verre dans ma poche."
concealed the glass in my pocket

"C'était   une   poudre   brillante..."
It was   a   powder   bright

"Le   lendemain,   comme   tu   venais   de   faire   les   petits
The   next day   as   you   came   from to make the   small

gâteaux,   je   les   ai   fendus   avec   un   couteau   et   j'ai   mis
cakes   I   them   have cracked   with   a   knife   and   I have set

le   verre   dedans..."
the   glass   there-in

"Il   en   a   mangé   trois...   moi   aussi,   j'en   ai   mangé   un....
He   of it has eaten   three   me   too   I of it have eaten   one

J'ai   jeté   les   six   autres   dans   l'étang...   les   deux   cygnes
I have   discarded the   six   others   in   the pond   the   two   swans

sont   morts   trois   jours   après....   Tu   te   le   rappelles? ...   Oh!
are   died   three   days   after   You   yourself it remember   Oh
(have)

ne   dis   rien...   écoute,   écoute....   Moi   seule,   je   ne   suis
not   say   nothing   listen   listen   Me   alone   I   not   am

pas   morte...   mais   j'ai   toujours   été   malade...   écoute....   Il
not   dead   but   I have always   been   ill   listen   He

est   mort...   tu   sais   bien..."
is   died   you   know   well
(has)

"Écoute...   ce   n'est   rien   cela....   C'est   après,   plus   tard...
Listen   this not is nothing that   It is   after   more   later

toujours...   le   plus   terrible...   écoute..."
always   the more   terrible   listen

"Ma   vie,   toute   ma   vie...   quelle   torture!   Je   me   suis   dit:
My   life   whole   my   life   what   torture   I   myself am   said
                                                                     (have)

Je   ne   quitterai   plus   ma   sœur.   Et   je   lui   dirai   tout,   au
I   not   leave   anymore   my   sister   And   I   her   will say   everything   at the

moment   de   mourir....   Voilà.   Et   depuis,   j'ai   toujours   pensé
moment   of   to die   That's it   And   since   I have   always   thought

à   ce   moment-là,   à   ce   moment-là   où   je   te   dirais   tout....
to   this   moment   there to   this   moment   there   where   I   you   would say   everything

Le   voici   venu....   C'est   terrible....   Oh! ...   grande   sœur!"
It   see-here   (has) come   It is   terrible   Oh   big   sister

"J'ai   toujours   pensé,   matin   et   soir,   le   jour,   la   nuit:"
I have   always   thought   morning   and   evening   the   day   the   night

"Il faudra que je lui dise cela, une fois.... J'attendais....
It will be needed that I her say that one time I waited

Quel supplice! ... C'est fait.... Ne dis rien..."
What torment It is done Not say nothing

"Maintenant, j'ai peur... j'ai peur... oh! j'ai peur! Si j'allais
Now I have fear I have fear oh I have fear If I went

le revoir, tout à l'heure, quand je serai morte.... Le
him see again all at the time when I will be dead Him
[soon]

revoir... y songes-tu? ... La première! ... Je n'oserai pas....
see again there dream you The first I will not dare not
[can you imagine] (As the) ()

Il le faut.... Je vais mourir.... Je veux que tu me
It it is necessary I go to die I want that you me
[It is necessary]

pardonnes. Je le veux.... Je ne peux pas m'en aller
forgive I it want I not can not myself from here go
()

sans cela devant lui. Oh! dites-lui de me pardonner,
without that in front of him Oh tell her of me to forgive

monsieur le curé, dites-lui... je vous en prie."
mr the priest say her I you of it pray
(beg)

"Je ne peux mourir sans ça..."
I not can die without that

Elle se tut, et demeura haletante, grattant toujours le
She became silent and remained breathing heavily scratching always the

drap de ses ongles crispés....
cloth of her fingernails clenched
(with)

Suzanne avait caché sa figure dans ses mains et ne
Suzanne had hidden her face in her hands and not

bougeait plus. Elle pensait à lui qu'elle aurait pu aimer
moved anymore She thought to him that she would have been able to love
(of)

si longtemps! Quelle bonne vie ils auraient eue! Elle le
so long What (a) good life they would have had She him

revoyait, dans l'autrefois disparu, dans le vieux passé à
saw again in the other times disappeared in the old past to
(for)

jamais éteint. Morts chéris! comme ils vous déchirent le
never extinguished Dead loved ones how they you would tear the
(ever)

cœur! Oh! ce baiser, son seul baiser!
heart Oh this kiss her only kiss

Elle l'avait gardé dans l'âme. Et puis plus rien, plus
She it had guarded in the soul And then more nothing more
(after that) (after that)

rien dans toute son existence! ...
nothing in all her existence

Le prêtre tout à coup se dressa et, d'une voix forte,
The priest suddenly stood up and of a voice strong
(tout à coup; all to strike) (with a)

vibrante, il cria:
rousing he called out

"Mademoiselle Suzanne, votre sœur va mourir!"
Miss Suzanne your sister goes to die

Alors Suzanne, ouvrant ses mains, montra sa figure
Then Suzanne opening her hands showed her face

trempée de larmes, et, se précipitant sur sa sœur, elle
soaked of tears and herself launched on her sister she
(in)

la baisa de toute sa force en balbutiant:
her kissed of all her force in stammering
(while)

71 La Confession

"Je te pardonne, je te pardonne, petite..."
I   you forgive   I   you forgive   little one

Émil   Zola   -   LE   CARNET   DE   DANSE
Emile   Zola   THE   NOTEBOOK   OF   DANCE
              [THE   BALLROOM   DIARY]

II
II

Georgette	sortait	à	peine	du	couvent.	Elle	avait	encore
Georgette	left	at [just]	pain	the	convent	She	had	still

cet	âge	heureux	où	le	songe	et	la	réalité
this	age	happy	where	the	dream	and	the	reality

se confondent;	douce	et	passagère	époque,	l'esprit	voit
themselves merge (merge)	sweet	and	fleeting	time	the mind	sees

ce	qu'il	rêve	et	rêve	ce	qu'il	voit.	Comme	tous	les
this	that it	dreams	and	dreams	this	that it	sees	As	all	the

enfants,	elle	s'était	laissé	éblouir	par	les	lustres	flambants
children	she	herself was (had herself)	let	dazzle	by	the	chandeliers	flaming

de	ses	premiers	bals;	elle	se	croyait	de	bonne	foi
of	her	first	balls	she	herself	believed	of (in)	good	faith

dans	une	sphère	supérieure,	parmi	des	êtres	demi-dieux,
in	a	sphere	higher	among	of the	beings	half gods

graciés	des	mauvais	côtés	de	la	vie.
pardoned (spared)	of the	bad	sides	of	the	life

Légèrement brunes, ses joues avaient les reflets dorés
Slightly brown her cheeks had the reflections golden

des seins d'une fille de Sicile; ses grands cils noirs
of the breasts of a girl of Sicily her great eyelashes black

voilaient à demi le feu de son regard. Oubliant qu'elle
veiled at half the fire in her look Forgetting that she

n'était plus sous la férule d'une sous-maîtresse, elle
not was anymore under the stick of an under mistress she

contenait la vie ardente qui brûlait en elle. Dans un
contained the life ardent that burned in her In a
(kept locked up)

salon, elle n'était jamais qu'une petite fille, timide,
salon she not was never (more) than a small girl shy

presque sotte, rougissant pour un mot et baissant les
almost foolish blushing for a word and lowering the
(at)

yeux.
eyes

Viens, nous nous cacherons derrière les grands rideaux,
Come on we ourselves will hide behind the great curtains

nous verrons l'indolente étendre les bras et s'éveiller en
we will see the indolent girl spread the arms and itself awake in

découvrant ses pieds roses.
discovering her feet pink

Ne sois pas jalouse, Ninon tous mes baisers sont pour
Not be not jealous Ninon all my kisses are for

toi.
you

Te souviens-tu? onze heures sonnaient. La chambre était
Yourself remember you eleven hours rang The room was

encore sombre. Le soleil se perdait dans les épaisses
still dark The sun itself lost in the thick

draperies des fenêtres, tandis qu'une veilleuse, aux lueurs
draperies of the windows while that a waker in the lights
(night light) (with)

mourantes, luttait vainement avec l'ombre. Sur le lit,
dying struggled in vain with the shade On the bed

lorsque la flamme de la veilleuse se ravivait,
where the flame in the night light itself revived

apparaissaient une forme blanche, un front pur, une
appeared a shape white a forehead pure a

gorge perdue sous des flots de dentelles; plus loin,
throat lost under of the waves of lace more further
()

l'extrémité délicate d'un petit pied; hors du lit, un bras
the end delicate of a small foot out of the bed an arm

de neige pendant, la main ouverte.
of snow hanging the hand opened
() (snow white)

A deux reprises, la paresseuse se retourna sur la
At two times the lazy girl herself turned around on the

couche pour s'endormir de nouveau, mais d'un sommeil
bed for to sleep in of new but of a sleep
[again]

si léger, que le subit craquement d'un meuble la fit
so light that the sudden creaking of a furniture her did
(of)

enfin dresser à demi. Elle écarta ses cheveux tombant
finally raise up herself at half She moved aside her hairs falling
() (halfway)

en désordre sur son front, elle essuya ses yeux gros
in disorder on her forehead she wiped her eyes big

de sommeil, ramenant sur ses épaules tous les coins
of sleep bringing on her shoulders all the corners

des couvertures, croisant les bras pour se mieux voiler.
of blankets crossing the arm for herself better to veil
(to cover)

Quand elle fut bien éveillée, elle avança la main vers
When she was well awake she forwarded the hand towards

un cordon de sonnette qui pendait auprès d'elle.
a cord of bell that hung close to of her

Mais elle la retira vivement; elle sauta à terre, courut
But she it withdrew lively she jumped at ground ran
(on) (the floor)

écarter elle-même les draperies des fenêtres. Un gai
pushing aside she herself the draperies of the windows A gay

rayon de soleil emplit la chambre de lumière. L'enfant,
ray of sun filled the room of light The child

surprise de ce grand jour et venant à se voir dans
surprised of this great day and coming to herself see in
(by)

une glace demi-nue et en désordre, fut fort effrayée.
a glass half naked and in disorder was hard scared
(windowpane)

Elle revint se blottir au fond de son lit, rouge et
She returned herself to snuggle in the back of her bed red and

tremblante de ce bel exploit. Sa chambrière était une
shivering of this beautiful feat Her chambermaid was a

fille sotte et curieuse; Georgette préférait sa rêverie aux
girl foolish and curious Georgette preferred her dreamy thoughts at the

bavardages de cette femme. Mais, bon Dieu! quel grand
chatter of this woman But good God what great

jour il faisait, et combien les glaces sont indiscrètes!
day it made and how much the glasses are indiscreet
(was) (windowpanes)

Maintenant,   sur   les   sièges   épars,   on   voyait   négligemment
Now   on   the   seats   scattered one   saw   carelessly

jetée   une   toilette   de   bal.   La   jeune   fille,   presque
thrown a   dress   of   ballroom   The   young   girl   almost

endormie,   avait   laissé   ici   sa   jupe   de   gaze,   là   son
asleep   had   left   here   her   skirt   in   gauze   there   her

écharpe,   plus   loin   ses   souliers   de   satin.   Auprès   d'elle,
scarf   more   further   her   shoes   of   satin   Next   of her

dans   une   coupe   d'agate,   brillaient   des   bijoux;   un   bouquet
in   a   cup   of agate   shining   of the   jewelry   a   bouquet

fané   se   mourait   à   côté   d'un   carnet   de   danse.
wilted   was dying   at   (the) side of a   book   of   dance
                                                  [ballroom   diary   ]

Le   front   sur   l'un   de   ses   bras   nus,   elle   prit   un   collier
The   front   on   the one   of   her   arms   nude   she   took   a   necklace
                    (one)

et   se   mit   à   jouer   avec   les   perles.
and   herself   set   to   play   with   the   pearls
      [started]

Puis elle le posa, ouvrit le carnet, le feuilleta. Le petit
Then she it put down opened the little book it leafed (leafed through) The small

livre avait un air ennuyé et indifférent. Georgette le
book had an air bored and indifferent Georgette it

parcourait sans grande attention, paraissant songer à tout
went through without great (a lot of) attention appearing to think to (of) all

autre chose.
other thing (things)

Comme elle en tournait les pages, le nom de Charles,
As she in turning the pages the name of Charles

inscrit en tête de chacune d'elles, finit par l'impatienter.
inscribed in head of each of them ended by her to make impatient

"Toujours Charles, se dit-elle. Mon cousin a une belle
Always Charles herself told she My cousin has a beautiful

écriture; voilà des lettres longues et penchées qui ont
writing see there of the letters long and thorough that have

un aspect grave."
an appearance serious

"La main lui tremble rarement, même lorsqu'elle presse
The hand him trembles rarely even when she presses

la mienne. Mon cousin est un jeune homme très-sérieux.
the mine My cousin is a young man very serious

Il doit être un jour mon mari. A chaque bal, sans
He must be one day my husband At each bal without

m'en faire la demande, il prend mon carnet et
me of it make the request he takes my book and

s'inscrit pour la première danse. C'est là sans doute un
inscribes himself for the first dance That is there without doubt a
()

droit de mari. Ce droit me déplaît."
right of husband This right me displeases

Le carnet devenait de plus en plus froid. Georgette, le
The book became of more in more cold Georgette the

regard perdu dans le vide, semblait résoudre quelque
look lost in the emptyness seemed to resolve some

grave problème.
serious problem

"Un mari," reprit-elle, "voilà qui me fait peur. Charles
A husband continued she see there which me makes fear Charles

me traite toujours en petite fille; parce qu'il a remporté
me treats always in (as a) small girl because that he has won

huit à dix prix au collège, il se croit forcé d'être
eight to ten prizes at the college he himself believes forced of to be

pédant. Après tout, je ne sais trop pourquoi il sera
pedantic After all I not know too much why he will be

mon mari; ce n'est pas moi qui l'ai prié de m'épouser;
my husband this not is not me who him has prayed of to marry me
(begged)

lui-même ne m'en a jamais demandé la permission. Nous
him self not me of it has never requested the permission we

avons joué ensemble, autrefois; je me souviens qu'il était
have played together before I me remember that he was

très-méchant. Maintenant il est très-poli; je l'aimerais mieux
very nasty Now he is very polite I him would like better

méchant. Ainsi je vais être sa femme; je n'avais jamais
nasty As well I go (am) to be his wife I not have never

bien songé à cela;"
good thought at (of) that

"sa femme, je n'en vois vraiment pas la raison. Charles,
his wife I not of it see really not the reason Charles

toujours Charles! on dirait que je lui appartiens déjà. Je
always Charles one would say that I him belong already I

vais le prier de ne pas écrire si gros sur mon carnet
go him pray of not not to write so large on my book

son nom tient trop de place."
his name holds too much of place

Le petit livre, qui, lui aussi, semblait las du cousin
The small book that to her too seemed weary of the cousin

Charles, faillit se fermer d'ennui. Les carnets de danse,
Charles failed itself to close van verveling The notebooks of dance
[almost closed]

je le soupçonne, détestent franchement les maris. Le
I it suspect despise frankly the husbands The

nôtre tourna ses feuillets et présenta sournoisement
our own turned its little pages and presented slyly

d'autres noms à Georgette.
of others names to Georgette
(other)

"Louis,"   murmura   l'enfant.   "Ce   nom   me   rappelle   un
Louis   whispered   the child   This   name me   recalls   a

singulier   danseur.   Il   est   venu,   sans   presque   me   regarder,
particular dancer   He   is   come   without almost   me   look at

me   prier   de   lui   accorder   un   quadrille.   Puis,   aux
me   pray   of   him   to grant   a   quadrille   Then   at the
     (ask)

premiers   accords   des   instruments,   il   m'a   entraînée   à
first   tunes   of the instruments   he   me has dragged   to

l'autre   bout   du   salon,   j'ignore   pourquoi,   en   face   d'une
the other end   of the salon   I do not know why   in   face   of a

grande   dame   blonde   qui   le   suivait   des   yeux.   Il   lui
big   lady   blonde   who   him   followed of the   eyes   He   her
                                                (with the)

souriait   par   moments,   et   m'oubliait   si   bien   que   je   me
smiled   at   times   and   forgot me   so   well   that   I   myself

suis   vue   forcée,   à   deux   reprises,   de   ramasser   moi-même
am   seen forced   to   two   times   of   pick up   my   self
(was)

mon   bouquet.   Quand   la   danse   le   ramenait   auprès   d'elle,
my   bouquet   When   the   dance   him   brought   close to   of her

il   lui   parlait   bas;"
he   her   spoke   low

"moi,   j'écoutais,   mais   je   ne   comprenais   point.   C'était
me   I listened   but   I   not   understood   nothing   It was

peut-être   sa   soeur.   Sa   soeur,   oh!   non   il   lui   prenait   la
maybe   his   sister   His   sister   oh   no   he   her   took   the

main   en   tremblant;   puis,   lorsqu'il   tenait   cette   main   dans
hand   in   trembling   then   when he   held   this   hand   in

la   sienne,   l'orchestre   le   rappelait   vainement   auprès   de
the   his   the orchestra him   reminded   vainly   next   of
()   (to)   ()

moi.   Je   demeurais   là,   comme   une   sotte,   le   bras   tendu,
me   I   was staying there   like   a   fool   the   arm   extended

ce   qui   faisait   fort   mauvais   effet;   les   figures   en   restaient
this   that   did   hard   bad   effect   the   figures   in   remaining
                                                               (dancing moves)

toutes   brouillées.   C'était   peut-être   sa   femme.   Que   je   suis
all   scrambled   It was   maybe   his   wife   What   I   am

niaise!   sa   femme,   vraiment,   oui!   Charles   ne   me   parle
silly   his   wife   really   yes   Charles   not   me   speaks

jamais   en   dansant.   C'était   peut-être..."
never   while   dancing   It was   maybe

Georgette resta les lèvres demi-closes, absorbée, pareille
Georgette remained (with) the lips half closed absorbed similar

à un enfant mis en face d'un jouet inconnu, n'osant
to a child set in face of a toy unknown not daring

approcher et agrandissant les yeux pour mieux voir. Elle
to approach and opening wide the eyes for better to see She

comptait machinalement sous ses doigts les glands de la
counted mechanically under her fingers the tassels of the

couverture, la main droite allongée et grande ouverte sur
duvet the hand right stretched out and wide opened on

le carnet. Celui-ci commençait à donner signe de vie; il
the book That one thereof began to give sign of life it

s'agitait, il paraissait savoir parfaitement ce qu'était la
fidgeted it appeared to know perfectly this that was the

dame blonde. J'ignore si le libertin en confia le secret
lady blonde I do not know if the libertine of it confided the secret

à la jeune fille.
to the young girl

Elle ramena sur ses épaules la dentelle qui glissait,
She brought back on her shoulders the lace that slipped

acheva de compter scrupuleusement les glands de la
finished of to count scrupulously the tassels of the

couverture, et dit enfin à demi-voix
duvet and said finally at half voice

"C'est singulier, cette belle dame n'était sûrement ni la
It is odd this beautiful lady not was surely nor the

femme, ni la soeur de M. Louis."
wife nor the sister of Mr Louis

Elle se remit à feuilleter les pages. Un nom l'arrêta
She herself again set to leaf through the pages A name her stopped

bientôt.
soon

"Ce Robert est un vilain homme," reprit-elle.
This Robert is a villainous man continued she

"Je n'aurais jamais cru qu'avec un gilet d'une telle
I / not would have / never / believed / that with / a / vest / of a / such

élégance, on pût avoir l'âme aussi noire. Durant un
elegance / one / could / have / the soul / so / black / During / a

grand quart d'heure, il m'a comparée à mille belles
large (long) / quarter / of hour (of an hour) / he / me has / compared / to / thousand / beautiful

choses, aux étoiles, aux fleurs, que sais-je, moi? J'étais
things / to the / stars / to the / flowers / what / know I / me / I was

flattée, j'éprouvais tant de plaisir, que je ne savais quoi
flattered / I felt / so much / of / pleasure / that / I / not / knew / what

répondre. Il parlait bien et longtemps sans s'arrêter. Puis,
to reply / He / spoke / well / and / long / without / himself to stop (stopping) / Then

il m'a reconduite à ma place, et là, il a manqué de
he / me has / led back / to / my / place / and / there / he / has / missed / of [he almost cried

pleurer en me quittant. Ensuite je me suis mise à une
to cry] / in / me / leaving / Next / I / myself / am / set / to / a

fenêtre; les rideaux m'ont cachée, en retombant derrière
window / the / curtains / me have / hidden / in / falling again / behind

moi."
me

"Je songeais un peu, je crois, à mon bavard de
I thought a bit I think at my talkative of ()

danseur, lorsque je l'ai entendu rire et causer. Il parlait
dancer whereupon I him have heard laugh and babble He spoke

à un ami d'une petite sotte, rougissant au moindre mot,
to a friend of a small fool blushing at the least word

d'une échappée de couvent, baissant les yeux,
of a breakaway of convent lowering the eyes

s'enlaidissant par un maintien trop modeste. Sans doute
herself disfiguring by a posture too modest Without doubt

il parlait de Thérèse, ma bonne amie. Thérèse a de
he spoke of Thérèse my good friend Thérèse has of ()

petits yeux et une grande bouche. C'est une excellente
small eyes and a big mouth It is an excellent

fille. Peut-être parlaient-ils de moi. Les jeunes gens
girl Maybe spoke they of me The young people

mentent donc! Alors, je serais laide. Laide! Thérèse l'est
lie then Then I would be ugly Ugly! Thérèse it is

cependant davantage. Sûrement ils parlaient de Thérèse."
however more Surely they spoke of Thérèse

Georgette sourit et eut comme une tentation d'aller
Georgette smiled and had as a temptation of to go
[felt tempted] (to go)

consulter son miroir. "Puis," ajouta-t-elle, "ils se sont
consult her mirror. Then added she they themselves are
(have)

moqués des dames qui étaient au bal. J'écoutais
mocked of the ladies that were in the bal I listened
bal

toujours, je finissais par ne plus comprendre. J'ai pensé
always I finished by not anymore understand I have thought
(all the time)

qu'ils disaient de gros mots. Comme je ne pouvais
that they said of big words As I not could

m'éloigner, je me suis bravement bouché les oreilles."
get away I myself am bravely plugged the ears
(have)

Le carnet de danse était en pleine hilarité. Il se mit à
The book of dance was in full hilarity It started to

débiter une foule de noms pour prouver à Georgette
reel off a crowd of names for to prove to Georgette

que Thérèse était bien la petite sotte enlaidie par un
that Thérèse was well the small fool made ugly by a
(indeed)

maintien trop modeste.
posture too modest

"Paul a des yeux bleus," dit-il. "Certes, Paul n'est pas
Paul has of the eyes blue said it Certainly Paul not is not
()

menteur, et je l'ai entendu te dire des paroles bien
(a) liar and I him have heard to you say of the words good
(the) (quite)

douces."
sweet

"Oui, oui," répéta Georgette, "M. Paul a des yeux bleus,
Yes yes repeated Georgette Mr Paul has of the eyes blues
()

et M. Paul n'est pas menteur. Il a des moustaches
and Mr Paul not is no (a) liar He has of the mustaches
() (a) (mustache)

blondes que je préfère beaucoup à celles de Charles."
blond which I prefer a lot to those of Charles

"Ne me parle pas de Charles," reprit le carnet; "ses
Not me speak not of Charles continued the book his

moustaches ne méritent pas le moindre sourire. Que
mustaches not deserve not the least smile What
(mustache) (deserves)

penses-tu d'Édouard? il est timide et n'ose parler que
think you of Édouard he is shy and not dares to speak but

du regard."
of the look
(by the) (looks)

"Je ne sais si tu comprends ce langage, Et Jules? il
I not know if you understand this language And Jules it ()

n'y a que toi, assure-t-il, qui saches valser. Et Lucien,
not there has but you assures he that knows (how to) waltz And Lucien
[there is no-one but you]

et Georges, et Albert? tous te trouvent charmante et
and Georges and Albert all you find charming and

quêtent pendant de longues heures l'aumône de ton
quest for of long hours the alm of your
()

sourire."
smile

Georgette se remit à compter les glands de la
Georgette herself set again to count the tassels of the

couverture. Le bavardage du carnet commençait à
duvet The chatter of the book began to

l'effrayer. Elle le sentait qui brûlait ses mains; elle eût
frighten her She it felt that burned her hands she had

voulu le fermer et n'en avait pas le courage.
wanted it to close and not for it had not the courage

"Car tu étais reine," continua le démon.
Because you was Queen continued the demon
(were)

"Tes dentelles se refusaient à cacher tes bras nus, ton
Your laces themselves refuse to hide your arms bare your

front de seize ans faisait pâlir la couronne. Ah! ma
forehead of sixteen years makes pale the crown Ah my

Georgette, tu ne pouvais tout voir, sans cela tu aurais
Georgette you not could everything see without that you would have

eu pitié. Les pauvres garçons sont bien malades à
had pity The poor boys are good ill at
(quite)

l'heure qu'il est!"
the time that it is

Et il eut un silence plein de commisération. L'enfant qui
And it had a silence full of commiseration The child who
[there was]

l'écoutait, souriante, effarouchée, le voyant rester muet;
it listened to smiled frightened it seeing stay dumb

"Un noeud de ma robe était tombé," dit-elle. "Sûrement
A node of my dress was fallen said she Surely
(had)

cela me rendait laide."
that me made ugly

"Les jeunes gens devaient se moquer en passant. Ces
The young people must themselves make fun in passing These
(must have) (made fun) (while)

couturières ont si peu de soin!"
seamstresses have so little of care
()

"N'a-t-il pas dansé avec toi?" interrompit le carnet.
Not has he not danced with you interrupted the book

"Qui donc?" demanda Georgette, en rougissant si fort
Who then asked Georgette in blushing so strong

que ses épaules devinrent toutes roses.
that her shoulders became all rose

Et, prononçant enfin un nom qu'elle avait depuis un
And pronouncing finally a name that she had since a

quart d'heure sous les yeux, et que son coeur épelait,
quarter of hour under the eyes and that her heart spelled
(of an hour)

tandis que ses lèvres parlaient de robe déchirée.
while that her lips spoke of dress torn

"M. Edmond," dit-elle, "m'a paru triste, hier soir. Je le
Mr Edmond said she me has appeared sad yesterday evening I him

voyais de loin me regarder. Comme il n'osait approcher,
saw from afar me watch As he not dared approach

je me suis levée, je suis allée à lui. Il a bien été
I myself am raised I am gone to him He has well been
(have) (stood up) (have)

forcé de m'inviter."
forced of to invite me

"J'aime beaucoup M. Edmond," soupira le petit livre.
I love a lot Mr Edmond sighed the small book

Georgette fit mine de ne pas entendre. Elle continua
Georgette made expression of not not to hear She continued
()

"En dansant, j'ai senti sa main trembler sur ma taillé.
In dancing I have felt his hand tremble on my waist
(While)

Il a bégayé quelques mots, se plaignant de la chaleur."
He has stammered some word himself complaining of the heat

"Moi, voyant que les rosés de mon bouquet lui faisaient
Me seeing that the roses of my bouquet him made
(I)

envie, je lui en ai donné une. Il n'y a pas de mal
pleasure I him of them have given one It not there has not of evil

à cela."
to that

"Oh! non! Puis, en prenant la fleur, ses lèvres, par un
Oh no Then in taking the flower his lips by a

singulier hasard, se sont trouvées près de tes doigts. Il
particular chance themselves are found close of your fingers He

les a baisés un petit peu."
them has kissed a little bit

"Il n'y a pas de mal à cela," répéta Georgette qui
It not there has not of evil to that repeated Georgette who

depuis un instant se tourmentait fort sur le lit.
since a moment herself tormented much on the bed

"Oh! non! J'ai à te gronder vraiment de lui avoir tant
Oh no I have to you scold really of him to have so much

fait attendre ce pauvre baiser."
made await this poor kiss

"Edmond ferait un charmant petit mari."
Edmond would make a charming little husband

L'enfant, de plus en plus troublée, ne s'aperçut pas que
The child of more in more troubled not realized not that
()

son fichu était tombé et que l'un de ses pieds avait
her scarf was fallen and that the one of her feet had
(had)

rejeté la couverture.
rejected the duvet

"Un charmant petit mari," répéta-t-elle de nouveau.
A charming little husband repeated she of again
[again]

"Moi, je l'aime bien," reprit le tentateur. "Si j'étais à ta
Me I love him well continued the tempter If I was at your
(quite)

place, vois-tu, je lui rendrais volontiers son baiser."
place see you I him would give back willingly his kiss

Georgette fut scandalisée.
Georgette was scandalized
(shocked)

Le bon apôtre continua
The good apostle continued

"Rien qu'un baiser, là, doucement sur son nom. Je ne
Nothing but a kiss there softly on his name I not

le lui dirai pas."
it him will say not
()

La jeune fille jura ses grands dieux qu'elle n'en ferait
The young girl swore her great gods that she not of it would do

rien. Et, je ne sais comment, la page se trouva sous
nothing And I not know how the page itself found under

ses lèvres. Elle n'en sut rien elle-même. Tout en
her lips She not of it knew nothing her self All while

protestant, elle baisa le nom à deux reprises.
protesting she kissed the name at two times
()

Alors, elle aperçut son pied, qui riait dans un rayon
Then she perceived her foot that laughed in a ray

de soleil. Confuse, elle ramenait la couverture, quand elle
of sun Confused she reapplied the duvet when she

acheva de perdre la tête en entendant crier la clef
finished of to lose the head in hearing screeching the key

dans la serrure.
in the lock

Le   carnet   de   danse   se   glissa   parmi   les   dentelles   et
The   book   of   dance   itself   slipped   among   the   laces   and

disparut   en   toute   hâte   sous   l'oreiller.
disappeared   in   all   hurry   under   the pillow

C'était   la   chambrière.
It was   the   chambermaid

99   Le Carnet De Danse

Guy de Maupassant - SOUVENIR
Guy de Maupassant   MEMORY

Comme il m'en vient des souvenirs de jeunesse sous la
How it me of it comes of the memories of youth under the
(come)

douce caresse du premier soleil! Il est un âge où tout
sweet caress of the first sun It is an age where all

est bon, gai, charmant, grisant. Qu'ils sont exquis les
is good gay charming exhilarating How they are exquisite the

souvenirs des anciens printemps!
memories of the old springs

Vous rappelez-vous, vieux amis, mes frères, ces années
You remember you old friends my brothers these years

de joie où la vie n'était qu'un triomphe et qu'un rire?
of joy where the life not was (more) than a triumph and than a laugh

Vous rappelez-vous les jours de vagabondage autour de
You remember you the days of vagrancy around of

Paris, notre radieuse pauvreté, nos promenades dans les
Paris our radiant poverty our walks in the

bois reverdis, nos ivresses d'air bleu dans les cabarets
woods green again our intoxications of air blue in the cabarets

au bord de la Seine, et nos aventures d'amour si
at the side of the Seine and our adventures of love so

banales et si délicieuses?
mundane and so delicious

J'en veux dire une de ces aventures. Elle date de
I of it want to tell one of these adventures. She (It) dates of

douze ans et me paraît déjà si vieille, si vieille, qu'elle
twelve years and me seems already so old so old that she
(years ago) (that it)

me semble maintenant à l'autre bout de ma vie, avant
me appears now at the other end of my life before
(of)

le tournant, ce vilain tournant d'où j'ai aperçu tout à
the turning this mean turning of where I have perceived all at
(of)

coup la fin du voyage.
strike the end of the trip
(a sudden)

J'avais — alors — vingt-cinq — ans. — Je — venais — d'arriver — à — Paris;
I had — then — twenty five — years — I — came — from to arrive — in — Paris
(I was) — — — — — [I just arrived   ]

j'étais — employé — dans — un — ministère, — et — les — dimanches
I was — employee — in — a — ministry — and — the — sundays

m'apparaissaient — comme — des — fêtes — extraordinaires, — pleines
appeared to me — as — of the — festivals — extraordinary — full

d'un — bonheur — exhubérant, — bien — qu'il — ne — se — passât — jamais
of a — happiness — exuberant — well — that it — not — happened — never
— — — (though) — (that there)

rien — d'étonnant.
nothing — of surprising

C'est — tous — les — jours — dimanche, — aujourd'hui. — Mais — je
It is — all — the — days — sunday — today — But — I

regrette — le — temps — où — je — n'en — avais — qu'un — par — semaine.
miss — the — time — where — I — not of it — had — than one — per — week

Qu'il — était — bon! — J'avais — six — francs — à — dépenser!
How it — was — good — I had — six — francs — to — spend

Je m'éveillai tôt, ce matin-là, avec cette sensation de
I myself early this morning there with this feeling of
() awoke

liberté que connaissent si bien les employés, cette
freedom that know so well the workers this

sensation de délivrance, de repos, de tranquillité,
feeling of deliverance of rest of tranquility

d'indépendance.
of independence

J'ouvris ma fenêtre. Il faisait un temps admirable. Le
I opened my window It made a weather admirable The
(was)

ciel tout bleu s'étalait sur la ville, plein de soleil et
sky everything blue was spread over the city full of sun and

d'hirondelles.
of swallows

Je m'habillai bien vite et je partis, voulant passer la
I dressed myself well fast and I left wanting to pass the
(very)

journée dans les bois, à respirer les feuilles; car je
day in the woods to breathe the leaves because I

suis d'origine campagnarde, ayant été élevé dans l'herbe
am of original countryside-man having been raised in the grass

et sous les arbres.
and under the trees

Paris s'éveillait, joyeux, dans la chaleur et la lumière.
Paris awoke cheerful in the heat and the light

Les façades des maisons brillaient; les serins des
The fronts of the homes shined the canaries of the

concierges s'égosillaient dans leurs cages, et une gaieté
janitors ego-whistled in their cages and a gaiety
(whistled showing off)

courait la rue, éclairait les visages, mettait un rire
ran through the street lit the faces put a laugh

partout, comme un contentement mystérieux des êtres et
everywhere as a contentment mysterious of the beings and

des choses sous le clair soleil levant.
of the things under the clear sun coming up

Je gagnai la Seine pour prendre l'Hirondelle qui me
I gained the Seine for to take the Swallow that me
(reached)

déposerait à Saint-Cloud.
would drop off at Saint Cloud

Comme j'aimais cette attente du bateau sur le ponton.
How I loved this awaiting of the boat on the pontoon

Il me semblait que j'allais partir pour le bout du
It me seemed that I went to leave for the end of the
(was going) (to)

monde, pour des pays nouveaux et merveilleux. Je le
world for of the countries new and wonderful I it

voyais apparaître, ce bateau, là-bas, là-bas, sous l'arche
saw appear this boat there down there down under the arch

du second pont, tout petit, avec son panache de fumée,
of the second bridge everything small with its plume of smoke

puis plus gros, plus gros, grandissant toujours; et il
then more big more big growing always and it

prenait en mon esprit des allures de paquebot.
took in my mind of the pretensions of freightship

Il accostait et je montais.
It docked and I stepped on

Des gens endimanchés étaient déjà dessus, avec des
Of the people in sunday best were already on top with of the
() (People)

toilettes voyantes, des rubans éclatants et de grosses
dresses showy of the ribbons brilliant and of large

figures écarlates.
faces scarlet

Je me plaçais tout à l'avant, debout, regardant fuir les
I myself placed all at the front upright watching flee the (move by)

quais, les arbres, les maisons, les ponts. Et soudain
docks the trees the homes the bridges And suddenly

j'apercevais le grand viaduc du Point-du-Jour qui barrait
I perceived the big viaduct of the Point of the Day that barred
(viaduc d'Auteuil in Paris)

le fleuve.
the river

C'était la fin de Paris, le commencement de la
It was the end of Paris the beginning of the

campagne, et la Seine soudain, derrière la double ligne
countryside and the Seine suddenly behind the twofold line

des arches, s'élargissait comme si on lui eût rendu
of the arches widened as though one her had rendered (given over)

l'espace et la liberté, devenait tout à coup le beau
the space and the freedom became all at kick (once) the beautiful

fleuve paisible qui va couler à travers les plaines, au
river peaceful that goes to flow through the plains at the

pied des collines boisées, au milieu des champs, au
foot of hills wooded in the middle of the fields at the

bord des forêts.
edge of the forests

Après avoir passé entre deux îles, l'Hirondelle suivit un
After to have passed between two islands the Swallow followed a

coteau tournant dont la verdure était pleine de maisons
hillside turning of which the greenery was full of homes

blanches. Une voix annonça: "Bas-Meudon", puis plus
white A voice announced Lower Meudon then more

loin: "Sèvres", et, plus loin encore "Saint-Cloud."
further Sèvres and more further still Saint Cloud

Je descendis. Et je suivis à pas pressés, à travers la
I went down And I followed at steps hurried through the

petite ville, la route qui gagne les bois. J'avais emporté
small city the road that gains the woods I had taken along
(reaches)

une carte des environs de Paris pour ne point me
a map of the surroundings of Paris for not in any case me

perdre dans les chemins qui traversent en tous sens
lose in the paths that traverse in all directions

ces petites forêts où se promènent les Parisiens.
these small forests where themselves walk the Parisians
(walk)

Dès que je fus à l'ombre, j'étudiai mon itinéraire qui
From when that I was at the shade I studied my itinerary that
(in)

me parut d'ailleurs d'une simplicité parfaite. J'allais tourner
me appeared from elsewhere of a simplicity perfect I went to turn
(by the way)

à droite, puis à gauche, puis encore à gauche, et
to (the) right then to (the) left then again to (the) left and

j'arriverais à Versailles à la nuit, pour dîner.
I would arrive at Versailles at the night for to dine
(to have dinner)

Et je me mis à marcher lentement, sous les feuilles
And I myself set to walk slowly under the leaves
[I started]

nouvelles, buvant cet air savoureux que parfument les
new drinking this air tasty that perfume the

bourgeons et les sèves. J'allais à petits pas, oublieux
buds and the saps I went at small steps forgetful
(I was going) (forgetting)

des paperasses, du bureau, du chef, des collègues, des
of the papers of the office of the chef of the colleagues of the
(the) (the) (the) (the)

dossiers, et songeant à des choses heureuses qui ne
archives and thinking to of the things happy that not
()

pouvaient manquer de m'arriver, à tout l'inconnu voilé de
could miss of to happen to me at all the unknown veiled of
(in) (by)

l'avenir.
the future

J'étais traversé par mille souvenirs d'enfance que ces
I was / traversed / by / thousand / memories / of childhood / that / these

senteurs de campagne réveillaient en moi, et j'allais, tout
scents / of / campaign / wake / in / me / and / I went (I was going) / all

imprégné du charme odorant, du charme vivant, du
impregnated / of the / charm / fragrant / of the / charm / alive / of the

charme palpitant des bois attiédis par le grand soleil de
charm / thrilling / of the / woods / warmed up / by / the / large / sun / of

juin.
june

Parfois, je m'asseyais pour regarder, le long d'un talus,
Sometimes / I / sat down / for / to watch / the / length / of a / slope

toutes sortes de petites fleurs dont je savais les noms
all / kinds / of / small / flowers / of which / I / knew / the / names

depuis longtemps. Je les reconnaissais toutes comme si
since / long / I / them / recognized / all / as / if

elles eussent été justement celles mêmes vues autrefois
they / had / been / precisely / those / same / seen / other times

au pays.
at the / countryside

Elles   étaient   jaunes,   rouges,   violettes,   fines,   mignonnes,
They   were   yellow   red   violet   fine   cute

montées   sur   de   longues   tiges   ou   collées   contre   terre.
perched   on   of   long   stems   or   pasted   against   earth
        ()

Des   insectes   de   toutes   couleurs   et   de   toutes   formes,
Of the   insects   of   all   colors   and   of   all   forms

trapus,   allongés,   extraordinaires   de   construction,   des
stocky   lengthened   extraordinary   of   construction   of the
        (long)

monstres   effroyables   et   microscopiques,   faisaient   paisiblement
monsters   appalling   and   microscopic   did   peacefully

des   ascensions   de   brins   d'herbe   qui   ployaient   sous   leur
of the   ascents   of   strands   of grass   that   sagged   under   their

poids.
weight

Puis   je   dormis   quelques   heures   dans   un   fossé,   et   je
Then   I   slept   some   hours   in   a   ditch   and   I

repartis   reposé,   fortifié   par   ce   somme.
left again   rested   fortified   by   this   sleep

Devant moi, s'ouvrit une ravissante allée, dont le feuillage
In front of me itself opened a very beautiful walkway of which the foliage

un peu grêle laissait pleuvoir partout sur le sol des
a bit sparse let rain everywhere on the ground of the

gouttes de soleil qui illuminaient des marguerites blanches.
drops of sun which illuminated of the daisies white
(the)

Elle s'allongeait interminablement, vide et calme. Seul, un
It stretched itself out interminably empty and calm Only a
(stretched in the distance)

gros frelon solitaire et bourdonnant la suivait, s'arrêtant
big hornet lonely and buzzing it followed stopping

parfois pour boire une fleur qui se penchait sous lui,
sometimes for to drink a flower that itself bent under it

et repartant presque aussitôt pour se reposer encore un
and moving off again almost immediately for itself to rest yet a

peu plus loin. Son corps énorme semblait en velours
bit more further Its body huge seemed in velvet
(of)

brun rayé de jaune, porté par des ailes transparentes et
brown striped of yellow carried by of the wings transparent and
()

démesurément petites.
inordinately small

Mais (But) **tout** (all) **à** (at / of) **coup** (strike / a sudden) **j'aperçus** (I perceived) **au** (at the) **bout** (end) **de** (of) **l'allée** (the walkway) **deux** (two)

personnes, (people) **un** (a) **homme** (man) **et** (and) **une** (a) **femme,** (woman) **qui** (that) **venaient,** (came) **vers** (towards)

moi. (me) **Ennuyé** (Annoyed) **d'être** (to be) **troublé** (troubled) **dans** (in) **ma** (my) **promenade** (walk) **tranquille** (quiet)

j'allais (I went / was going) **m'enfoncer** (to bury myself) **dans** (in) **les** (the) **taillis,** (thickets) **quand** (when) **il** (it) **me** (me) **sembla** (seemed)

qu'on (that one / that they) **m'appelait.** (called me) **La** (The) **femme** (woman) **en** (in) **effet** (effect) **agitait** (waved) **son** (her) **ombrelle,** (umbrella)

et (and) **l'homme,** (the man) **en** (in) **manches** (sleeves) **de** (of) **chemise,** (shirt) **la** (the) **redingote** (coat) **sur** (on)

un (the) **bras,** (arm) **élevait** (lifted) **l'autre** (the other) **en** (in) **signe** (sign) **de** (of) **détresse.** (distress)

J'allai (I went) **vers** (towards) **eux.** (them) **Ils** (They) **marchaient** (walked) **d'une** (of a / at a) **allure** (speed) **pressée,** (pressed / hastened) **très** (very)

rouges (red) **tous** (all / both) **deux,** (two) **elle** (she) **à** (at) **petits** (small) **pas** (steps) **rapides,** (rapid) **lui** (he) **à** (at)

longues (long) **enjambées.** (strides)

On voyait sur leur visage de la mauvaise humeur et
One saw on their face in the bad mood and

de la fatigue.
of the fatigue

La femme aussitôt me demanda:
The woman immediately me asked

"Monsieur, pouvez-vous me dire où nous sommes? mon
Sir can you me say where we are my

imbécile de mari nous a perdus en prétendant connaître
fool of (a) husband us has lost in pretending to know

parfaitement ce pays."
perfectly this country

Je répondis avec assurance:
I replied with assurance

"Madame, vous allez vers Saint-Cloud et vous tournez le
Madame you go towards Saint Cloud and you turn the
(are going) (have turned)

dos à Versailles."
back to Versailles

Elle reprit, avec un regard de pitié irritée pour son
She continued with a look of pity irritated for her

époux:
husband

"Comment! nous tournons le dos à Versailles. Mais c'est
How we turn the back to Versailles But that is

justement là que nous voulons dîner."
precisely there that we want to dine
(to have dinner)

"Moi aussi, madame, j'y vais."
Me too madame I there go

Elle prononça plusieurs fois, en haussant les épaules:
She uttered several times in shrugging the shoulders

"Mon Dieu, mon Dieu, mon Dieu!" avec ce ton de
My God my God my God with this tone of

souverain mépris qu'ont les femmes pour exprimer leur
sovereign contempt that have the women for to express their

exaspération.
exasperation

Elle était toute jeune, jolie, brune, avec une ombre de
She was all young pretty brunette with a shade of
(hint)

moustache sur les lèvres.
mustache on the lips
(upperlip)

Quant à lui, il suait et s'essuyait le front. C'était
As to him he sweated and wiped himself the forehead It was

assurément un ménage de petits bourgeois parisiens.
surely a household of small bourgeois Parisians

L'homme semblait atterré, éreinté et désolé.
The man seemed appalled frazzled and sorry

Il murmura:
He whispered

"Mais, ma bonne amie... c'est toi..."
But my good friend it is you

Elle ne le laissa pas achever:
She not him left not finish

"C'est moi! ..."
It is me

"Ah! c'est moi maintenant. Est-ce moi qui ai voulu partir
Ah / it is / me / now / Is / this / me / that / has / wanted / to leave

sans renseignements en prétendant que je me retrouverais
without / information / in / pretending / that / I / me / would find

toujours? Est-ce moi qui ai voulu prendre à droite au
always / Is / this / me / that / has / wanted / to take / to / (the) right / at the
()

haut de la côte, en affirmant que je reconnaissais le
height / of / the / coast / in / affirming / that / I / recognize / the
(river bank)

chemin? Est-ce moi qui me suis chargée de Cachou..."
road / Is / this / me / who / myself / am / charged / of / Cachou
(has) / (with)

Elle n'avait point achevé de parler, que son mari,
She / not had / not totally / completed / of / to speak / that / her / husband

comme s'il eût été pris de folie, poussa un cri perçant,
as / if he / had / been / taken / of / madness / pushed / a / cry / piercing
(let out)

un long cri de sauvage qui ne pourrait s'écrire en
a / long / cry / of / wild / that / not / could / be written / in
()

aucune langue, mais qui ressemblait à tiiitiiit.
any / language / but / that / seemed like / to / tiiitiiit

La jeune femme ne parut ni s'étonner, ni s'émouvoir, et
The young woman not appeared neither surprise herself nor move herself and
(to be surprised) (to be moved)

reprit:
continued

"Non, vraiment, il y a des gens trop stupides, qui
No really it there has of the people too stupid who
[there are] ()

prétendent toujours tout savoir. Est-ce moi qui ai pris,
claim always everything to know Is this me that has taken

l'année dernière, le train de Dieppe, au lieu de prendre
the year last the train of Dieppe in the stead of to take
(instead)

celui du Havre, dis, est-ce moi? Est-ce moi qui ai
the one of Le Havre say is this me Is this me that has

parié que M. Letourneur demeurait rue des Martyrs? ...
wagered that M Letourneur lived street of the Martyrs

Est-ce moi qui ne voulais pas croire que Céleste était
Is this me that not wanted not to believe that Celeste was
()

une voleuse? ..."
a thief

Et elle continuait avec furie, avec une vélocité de
And she continued with fury with a velocity of

langue surprenante, accumulant les accusations les plus
language surprising accumulating the accusations the most

diverses, les plus inattendues et les plus accablantes,
diverse the most unexpected and the more overwhelming

fournies par toutes les situations intimes de l'existence
provided by all the situations intimate of the existence

commune, reprochant à son mari tous ses actes, toutes
common reproaching to her husband all his acts all
()

ses idées, toutes ses allures, toutes ses tentatives, tous
his ideas all his aspects all his attempts all

ses efforts, sa vie depuis leur mariage jusqu'à l'heure
his efforts his life since their marriage up to the time

présente.
present

Il essayait de l'arrêter, de la calmer et bégayait:
He tried of stop her of her to calm down and stammered
    (to)   ()

"Mais, ma chère amie... c'est inutile... devant monsieur....
But my dear friend it is useless in front of (this) gentleman

Nous nous donnons en spectacle.... Cela n'intéresse pas
We ourselves give in (a) show That not interests not

monsieur..."
mr
(the gentleman)

Et il tournait des yeux lamentables vers les taillis,
And he turned of the (the) eyes dismal to them thickets

comme s'il eût voulu en sonder la profondeur
as if he had wanted of it fathom the depth

mystérieuse et paisible, pour s'élancer dedans, fuir,
mysterious and peaceful for to jump himself in there to flee

se cacher à tous les regards; et, de temps en temps,
himself hide at all the looks and from time in time
(hide) (from)

il poussait un nouveau cri, un tiiitiiit prolongé, suraigu.
he let go of a new call a tiiitiiit extended very sharp

Je pris cette habitude pour une maladie nerveuse.
I took this habit for a disease nervous

La jeune femme, tout à coup, se tournant vers moi, et
The young woman all at strike herself turning towards me and
(of) (a sudden)

changeant de ton avec une très singulière rapidité,
changing of tone with a very singular speed

prononça:
said

"Si monsieur veut bien le permettre, nous ferons route
If the gentleman wants well it allow we will make road
[will walk with him

avec lui pour ne pas nous égarer de nouveau et nous
with him for not not ourself lead astray of again and ourselves
] () ()

exposer à coucher dans le bois."
to expose to sleep in the woods

Je m'inclinai; elle prit mon bras et elle se mit à
I myself bowed she took my arm and she herself put to

parler de mille choses, d'elle, de sa vie, de sa famille,
talk of (a) thousand things of her of her life of her family

de son commerce. Ils étaient gantiers rue Saint-Lazare.
of her business They were glove-makers street Saint Lazare

Son   mari   marchait   à   côté   d'elle,   jetant   toujours   des
Her   husband   walked   at   (the) side of her   throwing   always   of the

regards   de   fou   dans   l'épaisseur   des   arbres,   et   criant
looks   of   crazy   in   the thickness of the   trees   and   calling out

tiiitiiit   de   moment   en   moment.
tiiitiiit   from   moment   in   moment
                             (to)

À   la   fin,   je   lui   demandai:
At   the   end   I   him   asked
(In)

"Pourquoi   criez-vous   comme   ça?"
Why   shout   you   like   that

Il   répondit   d'un   air   consterné,   désespéré:
He   replied   of an   air   appalled   desperate

"C'est   mon   pauvre   chien   que   j'ai   perdu."
It is   my   poor   dog   that   I have   lost

"Comment? Vous avez perdu votre chien?"
How (What) / You / have / lost / your / dog

"Oui. Il avait à peine un an. Il n'était jamais sorti de
Yes / It / had (was) / hardly / a / year (year old) / It / not was / ever / gone out / of

la boutique. J'ai voulu le prendre pour le promener
the / shop / I have / wanted / it / take / for / it / to walk

dans les bois. Il n'avait jamais vu d'herbes ni de
in / the / woods / It / not had / never / seen / of plants / nor / of

feuilles; et il est devenu comme fou. Il s'est mis à
leaves / and / it / is / become / as if / crazy / It / itself is set [has started] / to

courir en aboyant et il a disparu dans la forêt. Il faut
run / in () / barking / and / it / has / disappeared / in / the / forest / It / needs (One)

dire aussi qu'il avait eu très peur du chemin de fer;
to say / also / that it / had / had / very much / fear / of the / path [railroad / of / iron]

cela avait pu lui faire perdre le sens. J'ai eu beau
that / had / been able / him / to make / lose / the / sense (senses) / I have / had / nice (a lot)

l'appeler, il n'est pas revenu. Il va mourir de faim
it to call / it / not is / not / come back / It / goes (will) / die / of / hunger

là-dedans."
there in

La jeune femme, sans se tourner vers son mari,
The / young / woman / without / herself / to turn / towards / her / husband

articula:
uttered

"Si tu lui avais laissé son attache, cela ne serait pas
If you him had left his fastener that nto would be not

arrivé, Quand on est bête comme toi, on n'a pas de
happened When one is beast like you one not has not of
(dumb) ()

chien."
(a) dog

Il murmura timidement:
He whispered timidly

"Mais, ma chère amie, c'est toi..."
But my dear friend it is you
(it was)

Elle s'arrêta net; et, le regardant dans les yeux comme
She stopped cleanly and him watching in the eyes as

si elle allait les lui arracher, elle recommença à lui
if she was going them him tear out she began again at him

jeter au visage des reproches sans nombre.
throw at the face of the reproaches without name
(in the) ()

Le soir tombait. Le voile de brume qui couvre la
The evening fell The veil of mist that covers the

campagne au crépuscule se déployait lentement; et une
countryside at the dusk itself unfolded slowly and a

poésie flottait, faite de cette sensation de fraîcheur
poetry floating made of this feeling of freshness
( )

particulière et charmante qui emplit les bois à l'approche
particular and charming that fills the woods in the approach

de la nuit.
of the night

Tout à coup, le jeune homme s'arrêta, et se tâtant le
All at kick the young man stopped and himself fumbling the
(once)

corps fiévreusement:
body feverishly

"Oh! je crois que j'ai..."
Oh I think that I have

Elle le regardait:
She him watched

"Eh bien, quoi!"
Oh well what

"Je n'ai pas fait attention que j'avais ma redingote sur
I not have not made attention that I had my coat on

mon bras."
my arm

"Eh bien?"
Oh well

"J'ai perdu mon portefeuille... mon argent était dedans."
I've lost my wallet my money was in there

Elle frémit de colère, et suffoqua d'indignation.
She shook of anger and choked of indignation

"Il ne manquait plus que cela. Que tu es stupide!
It not missed more than that What you are stupid
[That was still missing] [You're so stupid]

Mais que tu es stupide! Est-ce possible d'avoir épousé
But what you are stupid Is this possible of to have married

un idiot pareil!"
an idiot equal

"Eh bien va le chercher, et fais en sorte de le
Oh well go it look for and make in kind of it
[do what's needed]

retrouver. Moi je vais gagner Versailles avec monsieur.
to recover Me I go reach Versailles with (this) gentleman

Je n'ai pas envie de coucher dans le bois."
I not have no lust of to sleep in the forest
()

Il répondit doucement:
He replied softly

"Oui, mon amie; où vous retrouverai-je?"
Yes my friend where you (I) will find I

"On m'avait recommandé un restaurant. Je l'indiquai."
One me had recommended a restaurant I it indicated

Le mari se retourna, et, courbé vers la terre que son
The husband himself turned around and curved towards the ground that his

œil anxieux parcourait, criant:
eye anxious ran over calling out
(looked over)

"Tiiitiit" à tout moment, il s'éloigna.
Tiiit / at / every / moment / he / walked away

Il fut longtemps à disparaître; l'ombre, plus épaisse,
He / was (took) / long / to / disappear / the shade / more / thick

l'effaçait dans le lointain de l'allée. On ne distingua
him erased / in / the / distance / of / the walkway / One / not / distinguished

bientôt plus la silhouette de son corps; mais on entendit
soon / anymore / the / silhouette / of / his / body / but / one / heard

longtemps son"tiiit tiiit, tiiit tiiit" lamentable, plus aigu
long / his / tiiit / tiiit / tiiit / tiiit / dismal / more / acute

à mesure que la nuit se faisait plus noire.
at measure (the more) / that / the / night / itself / made / more / black

Moi, j'allais d'un pas vif, d'un pas heureux dans la
Me / I went (I was going) / of a / step / lively / of a / step / happy / in / the

douceur du crépuscule, avec cette petite femme inconnue
gentleness / of the / dusk / with / this / small / woman / unknown

qui s'appuyait sur mon bras.
that / leaned / on / my / arm

Je | cherchais | des | mots | galants | sans | en | trouver. | Je
I | was looking for | of the () | words | gallant | without | of it | finding | I

demeurais | muet, | troublé, | ravi.
kept | silent | troubled | delighted

Mais | une | grand'route | soudain | coupa | notre | allée. | J'aperçus
But | a | highway | suddenly | cut | our | walkway | I saw

à | droite, | dans | un | vallon, | toute | une | ville.
at | (the) right | in | a | valley | all | a | city

Qu'était | donc | ce | pays.
What was | then | this | country

Un | homme | passait. | Je | l'interrogeai. | Il | répondit:
A | man | passed | I | him questioned | He | replied

"Bougival."
Bougival

Je   demeurai   interdit:
I   remained   stunned

"Comment   Bougival?   Vous   êtes   sûr?"
How   Bougival   You   are   sure

"Parbleu,   j'en   suis!"
Egad   I of it am

La   petite   femme   riait   comme   une   folle.
The   small   woman   laughed   as   a   crazy person

Je   proposai   de   prendre   une   voiture   pour   gagner
I   proposed   of   to take   a   vehicle   for   reach

Versailles.   Elle   répondit:
Versailles   She   replied

"Ma   foi   non.   C'est   trop   drôle,   et   j'ai   trop   faim."
My   faith   no   It is   too   funny   and   I have   too much   hunger

"Je suis bien tranquille au fond; mon mari se retrouvera
I am quite calm at the base my husband himself will find
[actually]

toujours bien, lui. C'est tout bénéfice pour moi d'en être
always well he It is all profitable for me of it to be

soulagée pendant quelques heures."
relieved for some hours

Nous entrâmes donc dans un restaurant, au bord de
We entered therefore in a restaurant, at the side of

l'eau, et j'osai prendre un cabinet particulier.
the water and I dared to take a small room private

Elle se grisa, ma foi, fort bien, chanta, but du
She herself intoxicated my faith quite well sang drank of the

Champagne, fit toutes sortes de folies... et même la
Champagne made all kinds of follies and even the

plus grande de toutes.
most big of all

Ce fut mon premier adultère!
This was my first adultery

Émile Zola - UN BAIN
Émile Zola   A   BATH

Je te le donne en mille, Ninon. Cherche, invente,
I you it(them) give in thousand(thousands) Ninon Seek invent

imagine: un vrai conte bleu, quelque chose de terrifiant
imagine a true tale blue some thing of () terrifying

et d'invraisemblable... Tu sais, la petite baronne, cette
and of implausible (unbelievable) You know the little Baroness this

excellente Adeline de C., qui avait juré... Non, tu ne
excellent Adeline of C. who had sworn No you not

devinerais pas, j'aime mieux te tout dire.
would guess not I love better you everything to tell

Eh bien! Adeline se remarie, positivement. Tu doutes,
So well Adeline herself remarries positively You doubt

n'est-ce pas? Il faut que je sois au Mesnil-Rouge, à
not is it (is) not It is necessary that I am in Mesnil Rouge at

soixante-sept lieues de Paris, pour croire à une pareille
sixty seven leagues from Paris for to believe in a similar

histoire.
history

Ris, le mariage ne s'en fera pas moins. Cette pauvre
Laugh the marriage not itself of it will do not less This poor
[Laugh, the marriage will not be less because of it]

Adeline, qui était veuve à vingt-deux ans, et que la
Adeline who was widow at twenty two years and that the

haine et le mépris des hommes rendaient si jolie! En
hatred and the contempt of the men rendered so pretty In

deux mois de vie commune, le défunt, un digne
two months of life communal the deceased a worthy

homme, certes, pas trop mal conservé, qui eût été
man certainly not too bad preserved who had been

parfait sans les infirmités dont il est mort, lui avait
perfect without the infirmities of which he is died her had
(has)

enseigné toute l'école du mariage. Elle avait juré que
taught all the school of the marriage She had sworn that
[everything to be learned] (about)

l'expérience suffisait. Et elle se remarie! Ce que c'est
the experience sufficed And she remarries This that it is
(was enough) [This is the story for us

que de nous, pourtant!
that of us though
]

Il est vrai qu'Adeline a eu de la malechance.
It is true that Adeline has had of the mischance
() () (bad luck)

On (One / [One) **ne** (not / does) **prévoit** (foresees / not foresee) **pas** (not) **une** (an / such an) **aventure** (adventure / adventure) **pareille.** (similar /]) **Et** (And) **si** (if) **je** (I) **te** (you)

disais (said) **qui** (who) **elle** (she) **épouse!** (becomes a wife of) **Tu** (You) **connais** (know) **le** (the) **comte** (count) **Octave** (Octave) **de** (of)

R., (R.) **ce** (this) **grand** (big) **jeune** (young) **homme** (man) **qu'elle** (that she) **détestait** (hated) **si** (so)

parfaitement. (perfectly) **Ils** (They) **ne** (not) **pouvaient** (could) **se** **rencontrer** (encounter) **sans** (without) **échanger** (exchange)

des (of the / ()) **sourires** (smiles) **pointus,** (sharp) **sans** (without) **s'égorger** (eachother slaughter) **doucement** (softly) **avec** (with) **des** (of the / ())

phrases (phrases) **aimables.** (friendly) **Ah!** (Ah) **les** (the) **malheureux!** (unhappy) **si** (if) **tu** (you) **savais** (knew) **où** (where)

ils (they) **se** (eachother are / (have)) **sont** **rencontrés** (encountered) **une** (a) **dernière** (last) **fois...** (time) **Je** (I) **vois** (see) **bien** (well)

qu'il (that it) **faut** (is necessary) **que** (that) **je** (I) **te** (you) **conte** (tell) **ça.** (that) **C'est** (It is) **tout** (all / (totally)) **un** (a) **roman.** (novel) **Il** (It)

pleut (rains) **ce** (this) **matin.** (morning) **Je** (I) **vais** (go) **mettre** (put) **la** (the) **chose** (thing) **en** (in) **chapitres.** (chapters)

I

Le Château est à six lieues de Tours. Du Mesnil-
The Castle is at six leagues from Tours. Du Mesnil

Rouge, j'en vois les toits d'ardoise, noyés dans les
Rouge, I of it see the roofs of slate drowned in the

verdures du parc. On le nomme le Château de la
greens of the park. One it names the Castle of the

Belle-au-Bois-dormant, parce qu'il fut jadis habité par un
Beauty at the Woods sleeping (Sleeping Beauty of the Woods) because that it was once inhabited by a

seigneur qui faillit y épouser une de ses fermières. La
lord that ended up there to marry one of his farm ladies. The

chère enfant y vécut cloîtrée, et je crois que son
dear child there lived cloistered, and I think that her

ombre y revient. Jamais pierres n'ont eu une telle
shadow (ghost) there returns. Never stones not had had a such

senteur d'amour.
scent of love.

La Belle qui y dort aujourd'hui est la vieille comtesse
The Beautiful who there sleeps today is the old countess

de M., une tante d'Adeline.
of M., an aunt of Adeline.

137   Un Bain

Il   y   a   trente   ans   qu'elle   doit   venir   passer   un   hiver   à
It   there   has   thirty   years   that she   must   come   to pass   a   winter   in
[It has been   thirty   years since   ]

Paris.   Ses   nièces   et   ses   neveux   lui   donnent   chacun
Paris   Her   nieces   and   her   nephews   her   give   each
(visit)

une   quinzaine,   à   la   belle   saison.
a   fortnight   in   the   beautiful   season

Adeline   est   très-ponctuelle.   D'ailleurs,   elle   aime   le
Adeline   is   very   punctual   Besides   she   loves   the

Château,   une   ruine   légendaire   que   les   pluies   et   les
Castle   a   ruin   legendary   that   the   rains   and   the

vents   émiettent,   au   milieu   d'une   forêt   vierge.
winds   break down   in the   middle   of a   forest   virgin

La   vieille   comtesse   a   formellement   recommandé   de   ne
The   old   countess   has   formally   ordered   of   not

toucher   ni   aux   plafonds   qui   se   lézardent,   ni   aux
to touch   neither   to the   ceilings   that   themselves crack   nor   to the
(are cracking)

branches   folles   qui   barrent   les   allées.
branches   mad   that   barred   the   walkways

Elle est heureuse de ce mur de feuilles qui s'épaissit
She is happy of this wall of leaves that thickens
(with)

là, chaque printemps, et elle dit, d'ordinaire, que la
there every spring and she says of usual that the
(usually)

maison est encore plus solide qu'elle. La vérité est que
house is still more solid than she The truth is that

toute une aile est par terre. Ces aimables retraites,
all a wing is on ground These friendly retreats
[a whole wing] [has collapsed]

bâties sous Louis XV, étaient, comme les amours du
built under Louis XV were as the loves of the
(during the reign of)

temps, un déjeuner de soleil. Les plâtres se sont
time a lunch of sun The plasters themselves are
(in the) (have)

fendus, les planchers ont cédé, la mousse a verdi
cracked the floors have yielded the moss has greened
[made green]

jusqu'aux alcôves. Toute l'humidité du parc a mis là une
up to the alcoves All the moisture of the park has set there a

fraîcheur où passe encore l'odeur musquée des tendresses
freshness where passes still the scent musky of the tenderness

d'autrefois.
of other times
(bygone days)

Le parc menace d'entrer dans la maison.
The park threatens of to enter in the house
(to enter)

Des arbres ont poussé au pied des perrons, dans les
Of the / () — trees / (Trees) — have — pushed / (grown) — to the — foot — of the — stoops — in — the

fentes des marches.
slots — of the — steps

Il n'y a plus que la grande allée qui soit carrossable;
It — not there has / [There is only — more — than — the — big — driveway — that — is — driveable by coach
] —

encore faut-il que le cocher conduise ses bêtes à la
still — it is necessary — that — the — coachman — leads — his — animals — at — the

main. A droite, à gauche, les taillis restent vierges,
hand — At — right / (the right side) — at — left / (the left side) — the — thickets — remain — virgin

creusés de rares sentiers, noirs d'ombre, où l'on avance,
crossed — of / (by) — rare — trails — black — of shade — where — it one / () — advances

les mains tendues, écartant les herbes.
the — hands — extended — pushing away — the — grasses

Et les troncs abattus font des impasses de ces bouts
And — the — (tree) trunks — cut down — make — of the / () — impasses — of — these — ends

de chemins, tandis que les clairières rétrécies ressemblent
of — paths — while — that — the — clearings — narrowed — seem

à des puits ouverts sur le bleu du ciel.
to — of the / () — wells — open — onto — the — blue — of the — sky

La mousse pend des branches, les douces-amères tendent
The moss hangs from the branches the sweet-bitters stretch out
(climbing nightshade)

des rideaux sous les futaies; des pullulements d'insectes,
of the curtains under the forests of tall trees of the outbreaks of insects
() (there are the)

des bourdonnements d'oiseaux qu'on ne voit pas, donnent
of the hum of birds that one not sees not give

une étrange vie à cette énormité de feuillages. J'ai eu
a strange life to this enormity of foliage. I have had

souvent de petits frissons de peur, en allant rendre
often of small chills of fear in going to give
() (to make)

visite à la comtesse; les taillis me soufflaient sur la
(a) visit to the countess the thickets me blowed on the

nuque des haleines inquiétantes.
neck of the breaths disturbing

Mais il y a surtout un coin délicieux et troublant, dans
But it there has above all a corner delicious and troubling in
() (is)

le parc: c'est à gauche du Château, au bout d'un
the park it is at the left of the Castle at the end of a

parterre, où il ne pousse plus que des coquelicots aussi
parterre where it not grows more than of the poppies as
() ()

grands que moi.
large as me

Sous un bouquet d'arbres, une grotte se creuse,
Under a bundle of trees a cave itself hollows

s'enfonçant au milieu d'une draperie de lierre, dont les
sinking in the middle of a drapery of ivy of which the

bouts traînent jusque dans l'herbe. La grotte, envahie,
ends hang just down in the grass The cave invaded

obstruée, n'est plus qu'un trou noir, au fond duquel on
obstructed not is more than a hole black at the back of which one

aperçoit la blancheur d'un Amour de plâtre, souriant, un
perceives the whiteness of a Cupid of plaster smiling a

doigt sur la bouche. Le pauvre Amour est manchot, et
finger on the mouth The poor Cupid is one-armed and

il a, sur l'oeil droit, une tache de mousse qui le rend
he has on the eye right a stain of moss that it makes

borgne. Il semble garder, avec son sourire pâle d'infirme,
one-eyed It appears to watch with his smile pale of cripple
(of a cripple)

quelque amoureuse dame morte depuis un siècle.
some in love being lady dead since a century

Une eau vive, qui sort de la grotte, s'étale en large
A water lively that comes out of the cave spreads in (a) wide

nappe au milieu de la clairière; puis, elle s'échappe par
sheet in the middle of the clearing then she escapes by
(sheet of water) (it)

un ruisseau perdu sous les feuilles. C'est un bassin
a stream lost under the leaves It is a basin

naturel, au fond de sable, dans lequel les grands
natural on the bottom of sand in which the great
()

arbres se regardent; le trou bleu du ciel fait une tache
trees look at eachother the hole blue of the sky makes a spot

bleue au centre du bassin. Des joncs ont grandi, des
blue at the center of the basin Of the rushes have grown of the
() (Rushes) ()

nénufars ont élargi leurs feuilles rondes. On n'entend,
lilies have expanded their leaves round One not hears

dans le jour verdâtre de ce puits de verdure, qui
in the day greenish of this well of greenery that

semble s'ouvrir en haut et en bas sur le lac du
appears to open itself in above and in below on the lake of the
(to the)

grand air, que la chanson de l'eau, tombant
great air than the song of the water falling

éternellement, d'un air de lassitude douce.
eternally of an ambience of lassitude sweet

143 Un Bain

De longues mouches d'eau patinent dans un coin. Un
Of *long* *flies (mosquito's)* *of water* *skate* *in* *a* *corner* *A*

pinson vient boire, avec des mines délicates, craignant
lark *comes* *to drink* *with* *of the* *expressions* *delicate* *fearing*

de se mouiller les pattes. Un frisson brusque des
of *to wet himself* *the* *paws* *A* *breeze* *abrupt* *of the*

feuilles donne à la mare une pâmoison de vierge dont
leaves *gives* *to* *the* *pond* *a* *swoon* *of* *virginity* *of which*

les paupières battent. Et, du noir de la grotte, l'Amour
the *eyelids* *flutter* *And* *from the black (darkness)* *of* *the* *cave* *the Cupid*

de plâtre commande le silence, le repos, toutes les
of *plaster* *commands* *the* *silence* *the* *rest* *all* *the*

discrétions des eaux et des bois, à ce coin voluptueux
discretions *of the* *waters* *and* *of the* *wood* *at* *this* *corner* *voluptuous*

de nature.
of *nature*

II

II

Lorsque Adeline accorde une quinzaine à sa tante, ce
When Adeline grants a fortnight to her aunt this

pays de loups s'humanise. Il faut élargir les allées pour
country of wolves is humanized It is necessary to expand the walkways for (so)

que les jupes d'Adeline puissent passer. Elle est venue,
that the skirts of Adeline can pass She is (has) come

cette saison, avec trente-deux malles, qu'on a dû porter
this season with thirty two trunks that they has had to carry (from devoir; must)

à bras, parce que le camion du chemin de fer n'a
by arm because that the truck of the road of iron (railroad) not has

jamais osé s'engager dans les arbres. Il y serait resté,
never (ever) dared engage in the trees It there would be (would have) stayed

je te le jure.
I you it swear

D'ailleurs, Adeline est une sauvage, comme tu sais.
Besides Adeline is a savage as you know

Elle est fêlée, là, entre nous. Au couvent, elle avait
She is flaky there between us In the convent she had
(mad)

des imaginations vraiment drôles. Je la soupçonne de
of the imaginations really funny I her suspect of
()

venir au Château de la Belle-au-Bois-dormant pour y
to come to the Castle of the Beautiful in the Woods sleeping for there
(Sleeping Beauty of the Woods)

dépenser, loin des curieux, son appétit d'extravagances. La
to spend far away of the curious her appetite for extravagances The

tante reste dans son fauteuil, le Château appartient à la
aunt rests in her easy chair the Castle belongs to the

chère enfant qui doit y rêver les plus étonnantes
dear child who must there dream the most amazing

fantaisies. Cela la soulage. Quand elle sort de ce trou,
fantasies That her relieves When she goes out of this hole

elle est sage pour une année.
she is wise for a year

Pendant — During
quinze — fifteen
jours, — days
elle — she
est — is
la — the
fée, — fairy
l'âme — the soul
des — of the

verdures. — greens
On — One
la — her
voit — sees
en — in
toilette — dress
de — of
gala, — gala
promener — walk
des — of the ()

dentelles — laces
blanches — white
et — and
des — of the ()
noeuds — knots (bows)
de — of
soie — silk
au — in the
milieu — middle
des — of the

broussailles. — bushes

On — One
m'a — me has
même — even
assuré — assured
l'avoir — to have her
rencontrée — encountered
en — in
marquise — marquise (dressed as)

Pompadour, — Pompadour
avec — with
de — of
la — the
poudre — powder
et — and
des — of the
mouches, — snuffs
assise — sat

sur — on
l'herbe, — the grass
dans — in
le — the
coin — corner
le — the
plus — most
désert — desert
du — of the
parc. — park

D'autres — Other
fois, — times
on — they
a — have
aperçu — seen
un — a
petit — small
jeune — young
homme — man
blond — blonde
[a small young blond man]

qui — that
suivait — followed
doucement — softly
les — the
allées. — walkways
Moi, — Me
j'ai — I have
une — a
peur — fear

affreuse — awful
que — that
le — the
petit — small
jeune — young
homme — man
ne — not (no-one)
soit — is
cette — (than) this
chère — dear

toquée. — batty

Je sais qu'elle fouille le Château des caves aux
I know that she searches the Castle from the cellars to the

greniers. Elle furète dans les encoignures les plus noires,
granaries. She ferrets in the corners the most dark

sonde les murs de ses petits poings, flaire de son nez
probes the walls of her small fists sniffs of her nose
(with) (with)

rosé toute cette poussière du passé. On la trouve sur
pink all this dust of the past One her finds on

des échelles, perdue au fond des grandes armoires,
of the ladders lost in the back of the large cabinets
()

l'oreille tendue aux fenêtres, rêveuse devant les
the ear tense to the windows dreamy in front of the

cheminées, avec l'envie évidente de monter dedans et de
fireplaces with the envy evident of climbing up of-in and of
(there-in)

regarder. Puis, comme elle ne trouve sans doute pas
looking Then as she not finds no doubt not
(checking)

ce qu'elle cherche, elle court le parterre aux grands
this that she seeks she runs the parterre at the great
(with the)

coquelicots, les sentiers noirs d'ombre, les clairières
poppies the trails blacks of shade the clearings

blanches de soleil.
white of sun

Elle   cherche   toujours,   le   nez   au   vent,   saisissant   le
She   seeks   Always   the   nose   in the wind   catching   the

lointain   et   vague   parfum   d'une   fleur   de   tendresse   qu'elle
distant   and   vague   perfume   of a   flower   of   tenderness   that she

ne   peut   cueillir.
not   can   pick

Positivement,   je   te   l'ai   dit,   Ninon,   le   vieux   Château   sent
Positively   I   you   it have said   Ninon   the   old   Castle   smells of

l'amour,   au   milieu   de   ses   arbres   farouches.   Il   y   a   eu
the love   in the middle   of   her   trees   fierce   It   there has had
                                                   (wild)   [There has   been   ]

une   fille   enfermée   là   dedans,   et   les   murs   ont   conservé
a   girl   locked up   there in   and   the   walls   have   retained

l'odeur   de   cette   tendresse,   comme   les   vieux   coffrets   où
the odor   of   that   tenderness,   as   the   old   cabinets   where

l'on   a   serré   des   bouquets   de   violettes.   C'est   cette
the one has closed in of the bouquets   of   violets   It is   this

odeur-là,   je   le   jurerais,   qui   monte   à   la   tête   d'Adeline
odor there   I   it   swear   that   rises   to   the   head   of Adeline

et   qui   la   grise.
and   that   her   makes tipsy

Puis,	quand	elle	a	bu	ce	parfum	de	vieil	amour,
Then	when	she	has	drunk	this	perfume	of	old	love

quand	elle	est	grise,	elle	partirait	sur	un	rayon	de	lune
when	she	is	tipsy	she	leaves	on	a	ray	of	moon
										(of the)

visiter	le	pays	des	contes,	elle	se	laisserait	baiser	au
to visit	the	land	of the	(fairy)tales	she	herself	lets	kiss	on the

front	par	tous	les	chevaliers	de	passage	qui	voudraient
front	by	all	the	knights	of	passage	that	would like
(forehead)								

bien	l'éveiller	de	son	rêve	de	cent	ans.
well	to awaken her	of	her	dream	of	(a) hundred	years
				(sleep)			

Des	langueurs	la	prennent,	elle	porte	des	petits	bancs
Of the	languors	her	take	she	carries	of the	small	benches
()	(Languor)		(takes)			()		

dans	le	bois	pour	s'asseoir.	Mais,	par	les	jours	de
in	the	wood	for	to sit down	But	on	the	days	of

grandes	chaleurs,	son	soulagement	est	d'aller	se	baigner,
large	heats	her	relief	is	of to go	herself	bathe

la	nuit,	dans	le	bassin,	sous	les	hauts	feuillages.	C'est
the	night	in	the	basin	under	the	high	foliages	It is
								(foliage)	

là	sa	retraite.
there	her	retreat

Elle · She
est · is
la · the
fille · girl
de · of
la · the
source. · spring
Les · The
joncs · rushes
ont · have
des · of the ()

tendresses · tendernesses (tenderness)
pour · for
elle. · her
L'Amour · The Cupid
de · of
plâtre · plaster
lui · her [smiles
sourit, · smiles at her]
quand · when

elle · she
laisse · lets
tomber · down
ses · her
jupes · skirts
et · and
qu'elle · when she
entre · enters
dans · in ()
l'eau, · the water

avec · with
la · the
tranquillité · tranquility
de · of
Diane · Diane
confiante · confident
dans · in
la · the
solitude. · solitude

Elle · She
n'a · not has
que · but
les · the
nénufars · lilies
pour · for
ceinture, · belt
sachant · knowing
que · that
les · the

poissons · fish
eux-mêmes · themselves
dorment · are sleeping
d'un · of a
sommeil · sleep
discret. · discreet
Elle · She

nage · swims
doucement, · softly
ses · her
épaules · shoulders
blanches · white
hors · out
de · of
l'eau, · the water
et · and

l'on · it one
dirait · would call
un · a
cygne · swan
gonflant · swelling
les · the
ailes, · wings
filant · going by
sans · without
bruit. · noise

La · The
fraîcheur · freshness
calme · calms
ses · her
anxiétés. · anxieties
Elle · She
serait · would be
parfaitement · perfectly

tranquille, · quiet
sans · without
l'Amour · the Cupid
manchot · one-armed
qui · that
lui · her
sourit. · smiled at

151 Un Bain

Une nuit, elle est allée au fond de la grotte, malgré
One night, she is gone to the back of the cave in spite of

la peur horrible de cette ombre humide; elle s'est
the fear horrible of this shade humid she herself is

dressée sur la pointe des pieds, mettant l'oreille aux
stretched out on the point of the feet putting the ear to the

lèvres de l'Amour, pour savoir s'il ne lui dirait rien.
lips of the Cupid for to know if he not her would say nothing

III
III

Ce qu'il y a d'affreux, cette saison, c'est que la pauvre
This that it there has of frightful this season it is that the poor
[This that was frightful]

Adeline, en arrivant au Château, a trouvé, installé dans
Adeline in arriving at the Castle has found installed in

la plus belle chambre, le comte Octave de R..., ce
the most beautiful room the count Octave of R. this

grand jeune homme, son ennemi mortel. Il paraît qu'il
big young man her enemy mortal It seems that he

est quelque peu le petit cousin de la vieille madame
is some bit the small cousin of the old madame
[somewhat]

de M... Adeline a juré qu'elle le délogerait. Elle a
of M. Adeline has sworn that she him dislodges She has

bravement défait ses malles, et elle a repris ses
bravely undone her trunks and she has resumed her

courses, ses fouilles éternelles.
walks her searches eternal

Octave, pendant huit jours, l'a tranquillement regardée de
Octave during eight days her has quietly watched from

sa fenêtre, en fumant des cigares.
his window in smoking of the cigars
(while) ()

153 Un Bain

Le soir, plus de paroles aiguës, plus de guerre sourde.
The evening no more of words acute no more of war deaf (silent)

Il était d'une telle politesse, qu'elle a fini par le trouver
He was of a such politeness, that she has ended up by him finding

assommant, et qu'elle ne s'est plus occupée de lui.
boring, and that she not herself is anymore kept busy of (with) him

Lui, fumait toujours; elle, battait le parc et prenait ses
He smoked always she, beat (walked) the park and took her

bains.
baths.

C'était vers minuit qu'elle descendait à la nappe d'eau,
It was to midnight that she descended to the sheet of water

quand tout le monde dormait. Elle s'assurait surtout si le
when all the world slept. She herself assured above all whether the

comte Octave avait bien soufflé sa bougie.
count Octave had well blown out his candle.

Alors,   à   petits   pas,   elle   s'en   allait,   comme   à   un
Then   to   small   steps   she   herself of it   went   as   to   an
(with)

rendez-vous   d'amour,   avec   des   désirs   tout   sensuels   pour
appointment   of love   with   of   desires   totally   sensual   for
(very)

l'eau   froide.   Elle   avait   un   petit   frisson   de   peur   exquis,
the water   cold   She   had   a   small   chill   of   fear   exquisite

depuis   qu'elle   savait   un   homme   au   Château.   S'il   ouvrait
since   that she   knows   a   man   in the   Castle   If he   opened
(knows that there is)

une   fenêtre,   s'il   apercevait   un   coin   de   son   épaule
a   window   if he   saw   a   corner   of   her   shoulder
(little part)

à travers   les   feuilles!   Rien   que   cette   pensée   la   faisait
through   the   leaves   Nothing   but   this   thought   her   did

grelotter,   quand   elle   sortait   ruisselante   de   la   nappe,   et
shiver   when   she   came out   streaming   of   the   sheet   and

qu'un   rayon   de   lune   blanchissait   sa   nudité   de   statue.
that a   ray   of   moon   whitened   her   nudity   of   statue

Une   nuit,   elle   descendit   vers   onze   heures.
One   night   she   descended   to   eleven   hours

Le   Château   dormait   depuis   deux   grandes   heures.   Cette
The   Castle   slept   since   two   large   hours   This

nuit-là,   elle   se   sentait   des   hardiesses   particulières.   Elle
night there there she   felt   of the boldness   special   She

avait   écouté   à   la   porte   du   comte,   et   elle   croyait   l'avoir
had   listened to   the   door   of the count   and   she   believed   him to have

entendu   ronfler.   Fi!   un   homme   qui   ronfle!   Cela   lui   avait
heard   snore   Phew   a   man   that   snores   That   her   had

donné   un   grand   mépris   pour   les   hommes,   un   grand
given   a   big   contempt for   the   men   a   big

désir   des   caresses   fraîches   de   l'eau,   dont   le   sommeil
desire   of the caresses   cool   of   the water of which the   sleep
                                                                 (after which)

est   si   doux.   Elle   s'attarda   sous   les   arbres,   prenant
is   so   sweet   She   lingered   under   the   trees   taking

plaisir   à   détacher   ses   vêtements   un   à   un.   Il   faisait
pleasure   to   take off   her   clothes   one   by   one   It   did
                                                                       (was)

très-sombre,   la   lune   se   levait   à peine;   et   le   corps   blanc
very   dark   the   moon   itself rose   just   and   the   body   white

de   la   chère   enfant   ne   mettait   sur   la   rive   qu'une
of   the   dear   child   not   put   on   the   shore   but a

blancheur   vague   de   jeune   bouleau.
whiteness   vague   of   young   birch

Des   souffles   chauds   venaient   du ciel,   qui   passaient   sur
Of the   breaths   hot   came   from the sky that passed   on

ses   épaules   avec   des   baisers   tièdes.
her   shoulders   with   of the kisses   lukewarm

Elle   était   très   à   l'aise,   un   peu   languissante,   un   peu
She   was   very   at   the ease   a   bit   languid   a   bit
                           (ease)

étouffée   par   la   chaleur,   mais   pleine   d'une   nonchalance
stifled   by   the   heat   but   full   of a   nonchalance

heureuse   qui   lui   faisait,   sur   le   bord,   tâter   la   source
happy   that   her   made   on   the   edge   feel   the   source

du pied.
of the foot
(with the foot)

Cependant,   la   lune   tournait,   éclairait   déjà   un   coin   de   la
However   the   moon   turned   lit   already   a   corner   of   the

nappe.   Alors,   Adeline,   épouvantée,   aperçut   sur   cette
sheet   Then   Adeline   terrified   saw   on   this

nappe   une   tête   qui   la   regardait,   dans   ce   coin   éclairé.
sheet   a   head   that   her   watching   in   this   corner   lit

157 Un Bain

Elle se laissa glisser, se mit de l'eau jusqu'au menton,
She herself let glide herself put of (in) the water up to the chin

croisa les bras comme pour ramener sur sa poitrine
crossed the arms as for to take back on her chest

tous les voiles tremblants du bassin, et demanda d'une
all the sails trembling of the basin and demanded of a (with a)

voix frémissante:
voice trembling

"Qui est là? ... Que faites-vous là?"
Who is there What do you there

"C'est moi, madame," répondit tranquillement le comte
It is me madame replied calmly the count

Octave.... "N'ayez pas peur, je prends un bain."
Octave Not have no fear I take a bath

IV
IV

Il se fit un silence formidable. Il n'y avait plus, sur la
It itself did a silence great It not there had more on the
(There) () (fell) [There were no]

nappe d'eau, que les ondulations qui s'élargissaient
sheet of water but the ripples that widened

lentement autour des épaules d'Adeline et qui allaient
slowly around of the shoulders of Adeline and that went
(the)

mourir sur la poitrine du comte, avec un clapotement
to die on the chest of the count with a lapping

léger.
light

Celui-ci, tranquillement, leva les bras, fit le geste de
That one quietly lifted up the arms made the gesture of

prendre une branche de saule pour sortir de l'eau.
to take a branch of willow for to go out of the water

"Restez, je vous l'ordonne," cria Adeline d'une voix
Stay I you it order cried out Adeline of a voice
(with a)

terrifiée....
terrified

159 Un Bain

"Rentrez dans l'eau, rentrez dans l'eau bien vite!"
Go back in the water go back in the water well fast

"Mais, madame," répondit-il en rentrant dans l'eau jusqu'au
But madame replied he in returning in the water up to the

cou, "c'est qu'il y a plus d'une heure que je suis là."
neck it is that it there has more of an hour that I am there
[it's been more than one hour]

"Ça ne fait rien, monsieur, je ne veux pas que vous
That not makes nothing sir I not want not that you
(no difference)

sortiez, vous comprenez.... Nous attendrons."
go out you understand We shall wait

Elle perdait la tête, la pauvre baronne.
She lost the head the poor baroness

Elle   parlait   d'attendre,   sans   trop   savoir,   l'imagination
She   spoke   of waiting   without too much to know   the imagination

détraquée   par   les   éventualités   terribles   qui   la   menaçaient.
derailed   by   the   eventualities   terrible   that   her   threatened

Octave   eut   un   sourire.
Octave   had   a   smile

"Mais,"   hasarda-t-il,   "il   me   semble   qu'en   tournant   le   dos..."
But   ventured he   it   me   appears that in   turning   the back
                                              (that by)

"Non,   non,   monsieur!   Vous   ne   voyez   donc   pas   la   lune!"
No   no   sir   You   not see   then   not   the moon

Il était de fait que la lune avait marché et qu'elle
It was of fact that the moon had marched on and that she
[indeed]

éclairait en plein le bassin. C'était une lune superbe. Le
lit in full the basin. It was a moon superb. The

bassin luisait, pareil à un miroir d'argent, au milieu du
basin gleamed like in a mirror of silver in the middle of the

noir des feuilles; les joncs, les nénufars des bords,
black of the leaves; the rushes, the lilies of the edges
(on the)

faisaient sur l'eau des ombres finement dessinées, comme
made on the water of the shadows finely drawn as
()

lavées au pinceau, avec de l'encre de Chine.
washed in the brush with of the ink of China
()

Une pluie chaude d'étoiles tombait dans le bassin par
A rain hot of stars fell in the basin by
(through)

l'étroite ouverture des feuillages. Le filet d'eau coulait
the narrow opening of the foliages The thin line of water flowed
(foliage)

derrière Adeline, d'une voix plus basse et comme
behind Adeline, of a voice more low and as if
(with a)

moqueuse.
mocking

Elle   hasarda   un   coup   d'oeil   dans   la   grotte,   elle   vit
She   ventured   a   strike   of eye   in   the   cave   she   saw
                                  [glance   ]

l'Amour   de   plâtre   qui   lui   souriait   d'un   air   d'intelligence.
the Cupid of   plaster   who   (at) her smiled   of an   air   of intelligence
                                                             (with an)

"La   lune,   certainement,"   murmura   le   comte,   "pourtant   en
The   moon   certainly   whispered   the   count   however   in

tournant   le   dos..."
turning   the   back

"Non,   non,   mille   fois   non.   Nous   attendrons   que   la   lune
No   no   thousand   times   no   We   shall wait   that   the   moon
                                                                           (until)

ne   soit   plus   là....   Vous   voyez,   elle   marche.   Quand   elle
not   is   anymore   there   You   see   she   moves on   When   she

aura   atteint   cet   arbre,   nous   serons   dans   l'ombre..."
will have   reached   this   tree   we   will be   in   the shade

"C'est   qu'il   y   en   a   pour   une   bonne   heure,   avant
It is   that it   there   of it   has   for   a   good   hour   before
[It's   just that   it's   going   to be   more than an hour   ]

qu'elle   soit   derrière   cet   arbre!"
that she   is   behind   this   tree

"Oh!   trois   quarts   d'heure   au   plus....   Ça   ne   fait   rien.
Oh   three   quarters   of hour   at the   most   That   not   makes   nothing
                         (of an hour)

Nous   attendrons....   Quand   la   lune   sera   derrière   l'arbre,
We   wait   When   the   moon   will be   behind   the tree

vous   pourrez   vous   en   aller."
you   will be able   yourself   of it   to go

Le   comte   voulut   protester;   mais,   comme   il   faisait   des
The   count   wanted   to protest   but   as   he   made   of the
                                                                 ()

gestes   en   parlant,   et   qu'il   se   découvrait   jusqu'à   la
gestures   in   speaking   and   that he   himself   uncovered   up to   the
           (while)

ceinture,   elle   poussa   de   petits   cris   de   détresse   si   aigus,
middle   she   pushed   of   small   cries   of   distress   so   sharp
                   (let go)   ()

qu'il   dut,   par   politesse,   rentrer   dans   le   bassin   jusqu'au
that he   had to   by   politeness   go back   in   the   basin   up to the

menton.   Il   eut   la   délicatesse   de   ne   plus   remuer.   Alors,
chin   He   had   the   delicacy   of   not   anymore   stir   Then

ils   restèrent   tous   les   deux   là,   en   tête-à-tête,   on   peut
they   stayed   all   the   two   there   in   head   to head   one   can
              [both of   them   ]   [face to face]

le   dire.
it   say
(that)

Les   deux   têtes,   cette   adorable   tête   blonde   de   la
The   two   heads   this   lovely   head   blonde   of   the

baronne,   avec   les   grands   yeux   que   tu   sais,   et   cette
baroness   with   the   great   eyes   that   you   know   and   this

tête   fine   du   comte,   aux   moustaches   un   peu   ironiques,
head   fine   of the   count   at the   mustaches   a   bit   ironic
                            (with the)

demeurèrent   bien   sagement   immobiles,   sur   l'eau   dormante,
remained   good   wisely   immobile   on   the water   dormant

à   une   toise   au   plus   l'une   de   l'autre.   L'Amour   de   plâtre,
at   a   yardstick   at the   most   the one   of   the other   The Cupid   of   plaster
        (yardstick apart)

sous   la   draperie   de   lierre,   riait   plus   fort.
under   the   drapery   of   ivy   laughed   more   hard

V

V

Adeline s'était jetée en plein dans les nénufars. Quand
Adeline herself was thrown in full in the lilies When
(between)

la fraîcheur de l'eau l'eut remise, et qu'elle eut pris
the freshness of the water her had put back and that she had taken
(fixed up)

ses dispositions pour passer là une heure, elle vit que
her provisions for to spend there an hour she saw that

l'eau était d'une limpidité vraiment choquante. Au fond,
the water was of a clarity really shocking On the bottom

sur le sable, elle apercevait ses pieds nus. Il faut dire
on the sand she saw her feet bare It needs to say
(saying)

que cette diablesse de lune se baignait, elle aussi, se
that this she-devil of (a) moon itself bathed she too herself

roulait dans l'eau, l'emplissait des frétillements d'anguilles
rolled in the water filled it of the wriggling of eels

de ses rayons.
of her rays

C'était un bain d'or liquide et transparent. Peut-être le
It was a bath of gold liquid and transparent Maybe the

comte voyait-il les pieds nus sur le sable, et s'il voyait
count saw he the feet bare on the sand and if he saw

les pieds et la tête.... Adeline se couvrit, sous l'eau,
the feet and the head Adeline herself covered under the water

d'une ceinture de nénufars. Doucement, elle attira de
of a belt of lilies Softly she attracted of
(with a)

larges feuilles rondes qui nageaient, et s'en fit une
wide leaves round that swam and herself of them made a

grande collerette. Ainsi habillée, elle se sentit plus
large neckscarf Thus dressed she herself felt more

tranquille.
calm

Cependant, le comte avait fini par prendre la chose
Meanwhile the count had ended up by to take the thing

stoïquement.
stoically

N'ayant pas trouvé une racine pour s'asseoir, il s'était
Not having / not / found / a / root / for / himself to sit down / he / had

résigné à se tenir à genoux. Et pour ne pas avoir
resigned / to / himself / keep / at the / knees / And / for / not / to have

l'air tout à fait ridicule, avec de l'eau au menton, comme
the air / all / indeed / ridiculous / with / of / the water / to the / chin / as
( ) / (water)

un homme perdu dans un plat à barbe colossal, il
a / man / lost / in / a / dish / to / beard / colossal / he
(of)

avait lié conversation avec la comtesse, évitant tout ce
had / bound / conversation / with / the / countess / avoiding / everything / this

qui pouvait rappeler le désagrément de leur position
that / could / remember / the / inconvenience / of / their / position

respective.
respective

"Il a fait bien chaud aujourd'hui, madame."
It / has / made / well / hot / today / madame
(been) / (quite)

"Oui, monsieur, une chaleur accablante. Heureusement que
Yes sir a heat overwhelming Fortunately that

ces ombrages donnent quelque fraîcheur."
these shades give a freshness

"Oh! certainement.... Cette brave tante est une digne
Oh certainly This brave aunt is a worthy

personne, n'est-ce pas?"
person not is this not

"Une digne personne, en effet."
A worthy person in effect

Puis, ils parlèrent des dernières courses et des bals
Then they spoke of the past walks and of the balls

qu'on annonce déjà pour l'hiver prochain.
that one announces already for the winter next

Adeline, qui commençait à avoir froid, réfléchissait que le
Adeline who began to have cold thought that the
(be)

comte devait l'avoir vue pendant qu'elle s'attardait sur la
count must her have seen during that she lingered on the

rive. Cela était tout simplement horrible.
shore That was all simply horrible

Seulement, elle avait des doutes sur la gravité de
Only she had of the doubts on the gravity of

l'accident. Il faisait noir sous les arbres, la lune n'était
the accident It did black under the trees the moon not was
(was) (dark)

pas encore là; puis, elle se rappelait, maintenant, qu'elle
not yet there then she remembered now that she
()

se tenait derrière le tronc d'un gros chêne. Ce tronc
herself kept behind the trunk of a big oak This trunk

avait dû la protéger. Mais, en vérité, ce comte était un
had had to her protect But in truth the count was a

homme abominable.
man abominable

Elle le haïssait, elle aurait voulu que le pied lui
She him hated she would have wanted that the foot him

glissât, qu'il se noyât. Certes, ce n'est pas elle qui lui
slipped that he drowned Certainly this not is not she who him
() (her)

aurait tendu la main.
would have reached out the hand

Pourquoi, quand il l'avait vue venir, ne lui avait-il pas
Why when he her had seen come not her had he not

crié qu'il était là, qu'il prenait un bain? La question se
called out that he was there that he took a bath The question itself

formula si nettement en elle, qu'elle ne put la retenir
formed so clearly in her that she not could it retain

sur ses lèvres. Elle interrompit le comte, qui parlait de
on her lips She interrupted the count who spoke of

la nouvelle forme des chapeaux.
the new shape of hats

"Mais je ne savais pas," répondit-il;
But I not knew not replied he
[didn't know]

"Je   vous   assure   que   j'ai   eu   très-peur.   Vous   étiez   toute
I   you   assure   that   I had   had much fear   You   were   all

blanche,   j'ai   cru   que   c'était   la   Belle-au-Bois-dormant   qui
white   I have   believed   that   it was   the   Beautiful in the Woods sleeping   who
                                                        (Sleeping Beauty of the Woods)

revenait,   vous   savez,   cette   fille   qui   a   été   enfermée   ici....
returned   you   know   this   girl   who   has   been   locked up   here

J'avais   si   peur,   que   je   n'ai   pas   pu   crier."
I had   so much fear   that   I   not have   not   been able   to call out
                                                         ()

Au   bout   d'une   demi-heure,   ils   étaient   bons   amis,   Adeline
At the end   of a   half   hour   they   were   good   friends   Adeline

s'était   dit   qu'elle   se   décolletait   bien   dans   les   bals,   et
herself was   said   that she   herself   without-collar   well   in   the   balls   and
                                             (showed cleavage)

qu'en   somme   elle   pouvait   montrer   ses   épaules.   Elle   était
that in   sum   she   could   show   her   shoulders   She   was
                                                                             (had)

sortie   un   peu   de   l'eau,   elle   avait   échancré   la   robe
gone out   a   bit   of   the water   she   had   cut out   the   dress
                                                                         (lowered)

montante   qui   la   serrait   au   cou.   Puis,   elle   avait   risqué
rising   that   her   surrounded   to the   neck   Then   she   had   risked

les   bras.
the   arms

Elle ressemblait à une fille des sources, la gorge nue,
She resembled at a girl of the springs the throat bare
()

les bras libres, vêtue de toute cette nappe verte qui
the arms free dressed of all this cloth green that

s'étalait et s'en allait derrière elle comme une large
was spread and itself of it was going behind her as a wide

traîne de satin.
trail of satin

Le comte s'attendrissait. Il avait obtenu de faire quelques
The count softened He had obtained of to make some
(seen to it)

pas pour se rapprocher d'une racine. Ses dents
steps for himself get closer of a root His teeth
(to a)

claquaient un peu. Il regardait la lune avec un intérêt
clattering a bit He watched the moon with an interest

très-vif.
very lively

"Hein! elle marche lentement?" demanda Adeline.
Huh she goes slowly asked Adeline

"Eh! non, elle a des ailes," répondit-il avec un soupir.
Eh　not　she　has　of the　wings　replied　he　with　a　sigh

Elle se mit à rire, en ajoutant:
She　herself　put　to　laugh　in　adding
　　　[started]

"Nous en avons encore pour un gros quart d'heure."
We　of it　have　still　for　a　big　quarter　of hour
　　　　　　　　　　　　　　　[kwartier]

Alors, il profita lâchement de la situation: il lui fit une
Then　he　took advantage　cowardly　of　the　situation　he　her　made　a

déclaration. Il lui expliqua qu'il l'aimait depuis deux ans,
declaration　He　her　explained　that he　her loved　since　two　years
(declaration of love)

et que s'il la taquinait, c'était qu'il avait trouvé cela
and　that　if he　her　teased　it was　that he　had　found　that

plus drôle que de lui dire des fadeurs.
more　funny　than　of　her　to say　of the　tastelessnesses
　　　　　　　　　　　　　　　(tasteless compliments)

Adeline, prise d'inquiétude, remonta sa robe verte jusqu'au
Adeline taken by worry lifted up her dress green up to the

cou, fourra les bras dans les manches. Elle ne passait
neck stuffed the arms in the sleeves She not went

plus que le bout de son nez rose sous les nénufars;
more than the end of her nose pink under the lilies

et, comme elle recevait en plein la lune dans les
and as she received in full the moon in the

yeux, elle était tout étourdie, tout éblouie. Elle ne voyait
eyes she was all giddy all dazzled She not saw

plus le comte, quand elle entendit un grand barbottement
anymore the count when she heard a great splashing

et qu'elle sentit l'eau s'agiter et lui monter aux lèvres.
and that she felt the water move itself and her to come up to the lips

"Voulez-vous bien ne pas remuer!" cria-t-elle; "voulez-vous
Want you well not move called out she want you
(Would) (please) (don't) (would)

bien ne pas marcher comme cela dans l'eau!"
well not walk like that in the water
(please) (don't)

"Mais je n'ai pas marché," dit le comte, "j'ai glissé...
But I not have not walked said the count I have slipped
         (have)

Je vous aime!"
I you love

"Taisez-vous, ne remuez plus, nous parlerons de tout
Be silent you not move anymore we will talk of all
                 (don't)

cela, quand il fera noir... Attendons que la lune soit
that when it will do black (Let's) Wait that the moon is
                 (will be) (dark)   (until)

derrière l'arbre..."
behind the tree

VII
VII

La   lune   se   cacha   derrière   l'arbre.   L'Amour   de   plâtre
The   moon   itself   hides   behind   the tree   The Cupid   of   plaster

éclata   de   rire.
broke out   of   laughter
                (in)

177   Un Bain

The book you're now reading contains the paper or digital paper version of the powerful e-book application from Bermuda Word. Our software integrated e-books allow you to become fluent in French reading, fast and easy! Go to learn-to-read-foreign-languages.com, and get the App version of this e-book!

▶ ■ 2   Blanche Neige

BLANCHE-NEIGE

Il y avait un paysan appelé Ivan, sa femme se nommait Marie. Ces wife sans n'avaient pas d'enfants, et ils étaient très tristes.

The standalone e-reader software contains the e-book text, and integrates **spaced repetition word practice** for **optimal language learning**. Choose your font type or size and read as you would with a regular e-reader. Stay immersed with **interlinear** or **immediate mouse-over pop-up translation** and click on difficult words to **add them to your wordlist**. The software knows which words are low frequency and need more practice.

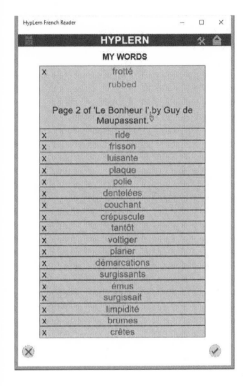

With the Bermuda Word e-book program you **memorize all words** fast and easy just by reading and efficient practice!

LEARN-TO-READ-FOREIGN-LANGUAGES.COM

je zons

(Je vous en prie, – I beg you to do it
"you're welcome"

Made in the USA
Monee, IL
07 May 2020